SHATTERED BY GRIEF

by the same author

Karuna Cards
Creative Ideas to Transform Grief
and Difficult Life Transitions
ISBN 978 1 78592 780 5

of related interest

Grief Demystified
An Introduction
Caroline Lloyd
Foreword by Dr Jennifer Dayes
ISBN 978 1 78592 313 5
eISBN 978 1 78450 624 7

Gone in the Morning
A Writer's Journey of Bereavement
Geoff Mead
ISBN 978 1 78592 355 5
eISBN 978 1 78450 691 9

Supporting People through Loss and Grief
An Introduction for Counsellors and
Other Caring Practitioners
John Wilson
ISBN 978 1 84905 376 1
eISBN 978 0 85700 739 1

The Essential Guide to Life After Bereavement
Beyond Tomorrow
Judy Carole Kauffmann and Mary Jordan
ISBN 978 1 84905 335 8
eISBN 978 0 85700 669 1

Effective Grief and Bereavement Support
The Role of Family, Friends, Colleagues,
Schools and Support Professionals
Kari Dyregrov and Atle Dyregrov
ISBN 978 1 84310 667 8
eISBN 978 1 84642 833 3

SHATTERED BY GRIEF
Picking up the pieces to become WHOLE again

CLAUDIA COENEN

Jessica Kingsley *Publishers*
London and Philadelphia

First published in 2018
by Jessica Kingsley Publishers
73 Collier Street
London N1 9BE, UK
and
400 Market Street, Suite 400
Philadelphia, PA 19106, USA

www.jkp.com

Library of Congress Cataloging in Publication Data
A CIP catalog record for this book is available from the Library of Congress

British Library Cataloguing in Publication Data
A CIP catalogue record for this book is available from the British Library

ISBN 978 1 78592 777 5
eISBN 978 1 78450 695 7

Printed and bound in Great Britain

For and because of Albert "Alby" George Coenen, Jr.,
my dancing partner for 26 years, who held me
in unconditional love to keep me whole.

And for Moke Mokotoff, my traveling partner
in our new adventure, who holds me with love
and Karuna as I continue to heal and grow.

David Byrne says, "This is not my
beautiful wife," to which I reply,

Yes I am.

Love

Alby

Contents

Preface and Acknowledgments

I have been a performer since I was four years old, and have always been comfortable on stage, in a crowd, in a circle of conversation. I have no problem telling an amusing story, acting it out with movement and changes of voice, often generating a laugh or nods of agreement. I love philosophical discussion and I love music, dance and especially human connection.

Because I am comfortable in public, talking with strangers, speaking what is on my mind, most people perceive me as an extrovert, and some even think I am a bit of an attention hog. While this may be partially true, at the core of my small person is a deeply introspective wonderer, concerned about why we are here on this planet. Even as a young teenager, I wanted to know the purpose of life, the purpose of relationships and the whys of nearly everything.

As I sit here in this latest phase of my life, I look back on many different manifestations of myself. At every turning, I have questioned the validity of what I was engaged in. I questioned the roots of the folk music I sang as a child and teen; I wanted to know how the song traveled with migrating people. I noticed the connections between lyric and melody and as a dancer, I noticed the connection between upbringing, history and even terrain on the types of movement in physical forms of expression. I wondered about it all.

Nothing prepared me for the catastrophic effects of grief. And even as I write that sentence, feeling its power and knowing the impact death had on my whole Self, I know it is simultaneously untrue. Everything prepared me to cope with the unspeakable horror of his death; even when I could not get out of bed there was a part of me that was wondering how to force myself to sit, swing one foot over the edge and step into the day. When everything felt misshapen including my body, when my heart felt squeezed into a tiny hard marble, I knew that somehow, sometime in the future, I would be able to feel complete again.

This book has been in process for 12 years, although its shape has morphed and its content has been enhanced by the experiences of other people experiencing death, not just me. As I write, I look back on the journals I have kept in the time of my own bereavement, in which I attempted to figure out the whys of this tragedy and what to do about it. I have also gone back to older books, mining those notebooks or at least the ones that have survived my 60 plus years of life.

What I find when I delve into my own musings is an overarching theme of connection, disruption and rebuilding. Starting again, beginning something new, trying different career paths and, more importantly, different modes of expressing my inner world, seems to be the leitmotif of my life. This book is an exploration of just that—my life was moving along in a fairly positive way when it suddenly imploded. Even in the midst of its devastation, I knew that I had to rebuild it and to try to make it even better than before.

I am so grateful to the people I love and who love me. I am grateful for my wonderful children, Chloë Coenen Mickel, Eben Coenen and Ilana Coenen. These three amazing humans also suffered an extreme loss at a young age and still have maintained their sense of wonder in the world. They each have used their pain to inform how they live and engage in the world. I see the influence of their father in their life choices. My sisters, particularly Jennifer Strohm and Maggie Hartley, have been my strength when I could not stand. Alby's sister, Nancy Coenen, even in the midst of her own deep sorrow over the loss of her brother, has helped enormously by continuing to be the loving aunt and another sisterly support for me. My youngest sister, Emily-Kate Niskey, has been an inspiration as she drew her way through her own struggle with breast cancer, choosing to remain positive with its aftermath. My dear brother, Jono Berger, and my other brothers, Bill Strohm, Dan Hannaburgh, and Forrest Hartley (in-law but brothers in fact), showed up, mowed the lawn, fixed things, hung out with the kids, represented Alby at important events, and sat with me many times, simply listening, even when I was silent. Everyone in our family—nieces, nephews, cousins, aunts, and uncles—loved Alby and were affected by his death. They rallied around me even when they did not necessarily know what to do or say.

I am grateful for my stalwart friends, Alice Nuccio, Riva Weinstein, Lori Patricola and Darrah Cloud. Not only did they hold me up, they also protected me. Lori and Alice arranged so many things I didn't even know about and thought were magically happening, like our meals which just arrived or extra staffing for my business, and most of the arrangement for the Celebration of Alby's life. Riva and I always share deep conversation about love and life, which keeps me sane. Darrah, who is a writer and a professor of creative writing, is always there to make me laugh or to pull together a ceremony or two and to edit my jumbled up work before I actually send it off to my editor.

Georgann Stewart and Eric Stand have always provided emotional sustenance to all of us since before the kids were born. I consider Georg my parenting guru; she listened and offered wisdom when I needed it. Eric's gentle, laconic and musical presence is always encouraging.

I'd also like to thank my two oldest friends, both Deborahs. I can't actually remember a time when I was not friends with Deborah Koff-Chapin, since we met when I was three. She has always been an inspiring force and her art expands my life. A pioneer in connecting soul and intuitive art, Deborah discovered her touch drawing process on her last day at Cooper Union when she was cleaning a lithograph plate. She travels the world conducting trainings, retreats and workshops in this deep process and I am proud to say I was there at its inception, when I would dance in her studio as she drew, fine tuning her new method of art-making. The eight touch drawings she sent me right after Alby died are so powerful I can only look at them for short periods of time. Deborah opens up compassion and creativity for people all over the world and I am so happy to have her as my friend. My other Deb, Deborah Mesibov, and I have been friends since we were five and share a bond that cannot be broken. She can look over at me and understand completely what I am thinking. She reminds me of who I am and where I have been because she has been there with me.

The shape of this book, while rooted in personal experience, would not be possible were it not for my mentors at the Institute of Transpersonal Psychology, Nancy Rowe, Anin Utegard, and Dorit Netzger. My professor at Brooklyn College, Dr. David Balk, encouraged me to pursue my career as a bereavement counselor and guided me towards certification through the Association of Death Education and Counseling. Thank you to Dr. Robert Neimeyer, who has been influential, in his theories, writing and teaching as well as providing personal encouragement.

I am also grateful for my mentors at Holy Name Hospice in New Jersey: social workers Amy Kotliar, Michelle Gardiner and Sandra Guzman, who taught me so much about counseling and sensitivity. All my colleagues challenged and supported me during the years we worked together to help our patients and their families. The spiritual counselors and the amazing nursing staff, especially at the Villa Marie Claire Hospice, enhanced what Alby had taught me about compassion. And thanks to Anne Lamana Smith, MA, who got me the job!

Thanks to Cait Johnson, who believed that I could write this book before I did. Gratitude to Bill O'Hanlon for his clear book proposal program and his endorsement of passionate writing.

I am grateful for the colleagues I have as a member of the loosely-knit Trauma Clinicians Group in Hudson, NY so that I can continue to learn and grow as a counselor. Working with traumatized clients is challenging and I am impressed by art therapist Sarah Mlynarczak's ability to remain positive in its face and for Adam O'Brien's passion for trauma resolution. Becky Sternal's commitment to working somatically with her clients is an inspiration. Psychologist Nancy Hoag has offered her expertise, warm support and friendship. Thanks also to my birthday twin, Jennifer Axinn-Weiss, whose wisdom combines her work as an artist, sand tray, hypnosis and Somatic Experiencing therapist.

My late husband Alby was a force of nature in his strong, quiet way. He was sensuous and sinewy; he loved to dance and he loved to dig in the earth, build stone walls and make things grow. His scientific mind and technical expertise were a mystery to me, and he actually enjoyed being a bit of an enigma. He started our family growing even when he was not quite ready for the responsibility of it. He lived up to his promise to participate consciously with me and our children. He cracked open a giant void when he left this world, but we fill it with our own commitment to continue his legacy and to create our own individual ones.

Last, I must acknowledge my love in this new phase of my life. Moke Mokotoff stepped out of his car on a warm summer day and nervously sat down on a park bench to wait for me, a person he had not met before. I knew almost immediately that we were connected, although I believe it took him a little longer to figure it out. His willingness to allow me to continue grieving even as we were falling in love helped me find ways to reconstruct my life. Moke has traveled with me all over the world, on planes, in cars, on chartered sailboats, and has introduced me to ideas I never explored such as art, antiquities, meditation and Tibetan Buddhism, from religious, philosophical and historical standpoints. He has introduced me to cultures I never knew about, to high lamas and Buddhist practitioners all over the planet as well as movers and shakers in the art world.

Together we have built an interesting life in a restored church, creating a welcoming home for children and friends to visit. His love and continued support make it possible for me to pursue and manifest my dreams.

Introduction

In May 2005, my husband Alby and I were in the 21st year of our marriage. We were in the thick of raising our three children, the oldest of which was about to complete her sophomore year at college. Our son was in eleventh grade and our little one was in eighth grade. For years my life had been consumed with augmenting the education of my children and driving them to all their activities, including field hockey, softball, soccer, art classes, dates and parties with friends and to years of swim meets, some of which were two hours away. In the midst of facilitating their expansion into their own lives, I was running my own catering business and rabblerousing for the PTA to stimulate better education for all children in our schools. I wrote and obtained grants to create a curriculum-based garden, and other grants to teach interpretive dance, one year turning the entire fourth grade into the Iroquois Nation. Meanwhile, Alby was increasingly consumed with work and participated as much as his limited time allowed. We tried to remember to nurture our connection to each other, which was becoming increasingly difficult since his high-tech job in the field of electron microscopy occupied him for longer and longer hours.

We had met through a newspaper ad, seeking housemates to rent rooms in a split-level house in the suburbs. Among other "requirements," the ad asked for people with lots of "joie de vivre." Alby and I independently called the homeowner and said the same thing. "I have lots of joie de vivre. I am just who you are looking for."

We became friends that year. He lived downstairs and I lived upstairs. He had just started his first job out of school, working for the only American manufacturer of electron beam microscopes. He learned how to fix them by spending a month at the factory, taking apart one of these giant, room-sized, technical behemoths and putting it back together again. This was in the early 1980s, back when mainframe computers were a thing and nanotechnology was hardly known outside the engineering world. I had quit my job and gone back to school to complete my Bachelor's degree in dance and literature.

Several years before this, my friend Deborah Koff-Chapin had introduced me to a spiritual teacher who used dance, drumming and earth-based imagery to create relevant rituals for our modern, disconnected times. This teacher was Elizabeth Cogburn, a social worker, belly dancer, and student of Native American religions and of Kabbalah, as well as the daughter of a gifted storyteller and an Episcopal priest. Her blend of sound, trance dancing, and moving meditation interested me and when Deborah invited me to bring a date to her wedding, officiated by Elizabeth, I brought Alby.

The ceremony began with all the guests hiking up a beautiful mountain trail, led by Elizabeth in white robes. We stopped at a plateau and a woman played a musical call on an oboe. From further up the mountain and from different points, the bride and groom, Deborah and Ross, walked towards each other, then continued down to the throng holding hands. Hoisting up the wedding quilt that many of us had contributed to, we continued to walk to a beautiful field. We hung the quilt on a giant tree as their canopy and, finally, the ceremony of their union commenced.

I do not remember the words that were spoken. I do remember feeling that this long hike, with each element of sound, smell and sight along the path, culminating in the drumming and wisdom imparted by Elizabeth, was a true expression of union. We as the community of friends and family were helping to weave Deborah and Ross together. I thought, this is what I want: to bond to a lover with conscious intention.

Alby and I were still only friends, but once I moved into the city to continue to dance, he began to visit me. Our attraction was so strong and finally, he asked if I would like to enjoy a summer romance. Our friendship shifted into love and our connection deepened. We married shortly before my 30th birthday in a ceremony we wrote ourselves, walking down the aisle in an infinity pattern. We circled together, then separated, came back together and separated again, all the while keeping our eyes on each other to demonstrate our respect for each other's independence and our intention to always share. He led one circle and I led another before we got to the last one where we took a step in unison.

In reflection on our relationship, I see the times of unity and closeness along with individuality in our different ways of being in the world. There were also times of difficulty and miscommunication, of struggle and challenge, but always, we came back together, circling closer until we understood each other. I am so grateful that we always found our way back to each other.

His death absolutely crashed my world. It took me a long time to believe it because it seemed so wrong, so unnecessary. The first few months of grief are blurry in my memory, as I alternated between intense emotion and dissociative numbness. I also had this odd sense of being outside of myself, noticing how I was handling this awful experience and thinking that maybe there was some method within it that could help others.

In the deepest, darkest time of my own anguish, I thought of becoming a grief counselor. I could not even imagine how to accomplish this goal, especially since I was so lost inside the turmoil of my own emotions, but I planted the seed in the summer of 2005. Slowly, I blazed my own trail towards that goal through study, volunteering and practice. As is typical for me, I did not take an ordinary or straight route towards my goal. It may have been easier to become a social worker or a mental health counselor, to come out of school with a known degree and a license. But I was focused. I did not want to learn how to navigate bureaucracy, although I sit in awe of those Masters of Social Work (MSWs) and licensed professional counsellors (LPCs) who are skilled at helping their clientele in so many important ways. I was bereft and I wanted to learn more about how to navigate the landscape of bereavement. And,

I thought if I learned more about it, I would find ways to cope. In terms of my budding idea to help others, it seemed that I knew how it felt to me but it would take a lot more education and insight into other situations if I wanted to help others who perhaps had been long-term caregivers for loved ones who were ill or who mourned other deaths and losses different than a spouse.

The Master's program I entered in transpersonal psychology has its roots in humanistic psychology, which holds that we can become more than the sum of our parts. Abraham Maslow, the grandfather of the humanist movement, believed that once our basic needs are met, we can aspire and grow to be fully actualized humans, able to respond in a more complete way. The transpersonal movement expands this idea to encompass our emotional responses, healthy psychology and our sense of spirituality, all of which combine to create our personhood. The transpersonal view includes peak experiences, which are beyond the personal, thus "trans-personal." It is a view that seeks to elevate the small personal one with goals and more transcendent possibilities. In some respects, transpersonal psychology may veer off into the far-flung fields of possibilities as it tends to include shamanism, holotropic breathwork, experimentation with psychotropic medications, and other out-of-mainstream psychological practice. On the other hand, there are currently many serious clinical studies done in hospitals in the USA right now on the effects of tiny doses of psychedelic medicines for people with cancer and other terminal illness, treating existential dread. The psychological treatment models for these studies are a direct outcropping of transpersonal psychology. Since transpersonal psychology openly endorses spirituality, it is sometimes referred to as "spiritual psychology."

I did not know any of this when I applied to the Institute of Transpersonal Psychology. What I did know is that I would not have to sit for the graduate school entrance exams, something that worried me since I was nearly 30 years out of college, plus I was still having trouble with my concentration, nearly three years after Alby's death. I knew the program was flexible and mostly online. This was beneficial since I had so much trouble sleeping; now I could go to school at 3 am instead of brooding and weeping. While I still struggled to read more than a paragraph at a time, I pushed myself to learn. I funneled every assignment through the lens of grief. I searched for grief counseling programs to enhance the Master's degree. I found one at Brooklyn College, where Abraham Maslow had taught and developed his psychological system. My thesis was called "Consider the Gifts" and explored the possibility of growth within loss. Coming back to wholeness was the focus of my grief, of my studies and, as it turns out, of my life. Becoming whole again after tragedy has become the inquiry of this book.

CHAPTER 1

From Shattering
to Wholeness

Death shatters you and breaks your life into little pieces. Well, this is not strictly true; not every loss is that extreme. I had experienced death before. A young friend died at 24, a close cousin died at 34. My grandparents died at 80, 87, 93 and nearly 101. I was sad, grieved deeply, especially after the death of my Oma. But nothing prepared me for how broken I would feel when my husband suddenly died while we were on vacation in New Mexico.

I never expected it; well, this also is not strictly true. I did expect that I would outlive him but I also expected that he would die in his 70s. Not four days after his 50th birthday. This catastrophe happened on a Tuesday night in May, the first time we had ever left our children home alone. This life-altering, split-second explosion in my relatively comfy life tilted everything, as if the ground beneath my feet had heaved and become stuck at a strange angle.

Suddenly I was not married. Suddenly I was alone. Suddenly I was a single mother in the middle of raising teenagers.

The thing is, even though we all know we will die someday, we act like it won't happen to us. I've had clients whose parents lived well into their 90s say, "I never thought she would die." We don't expect the death of someone we love, even if they suffer for years from a terrible disease. Even as we feed them sips of broth or beg them to eat just one little bite of the dinner we lovingly prepared for them, even as we sit with them in a hospice, we do not expect them to die. Given a 2 percent chance of survival, many people are certain their loved one will be in that slim margin. We watch them wither away, we hold their hand as their breath slows and still, and then we are in shock. There still is the unanswerable question. How could this be? Death feels wrong, so unfair. And afterwards, everything seems radically changed. Life as we expected it to be, as we projected it to be, is broken.

Nearly everyone feels a sense of shock initially after the death of a loved one. In my counseling practice, I have witnessed how difficult it is to accept the death, regardless of age or degree of illness. Because factors of relationship, family history, personality and support all feed into our grief reactions, each person's reaction is completely unique to them. There may be common themes: most people cry, have a sense of dislocation, feel numb or angry or both. But no two widows have exactly the same response to their husband's death; not every child whose elderly parent dies is stopped in their tracks. And parents whose child dies often have their grief experience magnified by the extreme injustice of a death at the wrong time. Not only do they mourn their child, they also mourn who they will never get to be, the experiences the child (and the parents) will never have. Of all losses, the death of a child is the most insuperable.

Psychiatrist Colin Murray Parkes, who assisted Cicely Saunders in founding the modern hospice movement in Britain, says that death shatters our *assumptive* world. We think we know how our life should be and then someone dies and it all falls to pieces. Our assumptions about where we are going, what we will do and even who we are evaporate. I did not know this theory when my husband died. But I certainly felt shattered. I felt as if the trajectory of my life had completely halted.

I also felt a compulsion to put myself back together again. It seemed imperative: If I was broken, I needed repair. If my life was in pieces, I had to find a way to rebuild it. And it also occurred to me that I could, perhaps, rebuild it in a subtly new way. It was not as if I was suddenly going to become a doctor or move to Borneo. But if I was shattered, I might be able to take a closer look at all the broken shards of my Self and consider them. Maybe there were strengths, skills, attributes that I could enhance. Certainly there were character aspects I'd like to diminish a little, if I could not rid myself of them outright. So my sudden dance with death did not have to mark the end of my life, although it was an end to my life as I knew it. Somewhere in the rubble, there were opportunities. Somewhere, inside the pain, so extreme it was almost physical, there had to be healing. Somehow, although I did not know how long it would take, I would find a way to grow from this calamity.

Humans are remarkable beings, complex mixtures of the physical, emotional, spiritual and psychological. Humanists have theorized that by integrating and enhancing these aspects of ourselves, we can become more than the sum of our parts. Abraham Maslow called this self-actualization. To me, it is a sense of wholeness, a balancing of these states into complete integration—an admirable goal but a difficult quest.

Grief affects us holistically, on all these levels of our being. The emotional reactions are obvious to everyone. Bereaved people feel mired in multiple emotions, pulling them in every direction, even as they feel numb and disconnected from others. People comment that they feel alone even in a group of caring people. Some use "unmoored" to describe the feeling of being suddenly adrift. Others talk about fear, anxiety. Sadness and bouts of crying rise up out of flashes of anger, injustice and disbelief. We sit in silence and we scream, all at the same time.

What are not so obvious are physical reactions such as stomach aches, inability to sleep and heart palpitations. Headaches and pains in the area of the heart are common. My body shook uncontrollably for weeks after Alby died, especially my legs. This was alarming to me and to my children, who watched me closely as if they were afraid I was coming apart in front of their eyes. Some people can't seem to get enough to eat; I did not notice hunger at all, and unless someone handed me food, I forgot to eat.

Concentration and cognition are affected. Loss is unruly, unsettling and out of control. Everything seems tilted, slowed or simply wrong. We long for "normalcy," we want our life back the way it was. The combination of fuzzy thinking and forgetfulness, along with fluctuating emotions, can make newly bereaved people worry that they are losing their minds. At about four months in, I actually thought I was mentally ill. Fortunately, I joined an online support group and was immediately reassured that this was a symptom of grief rather than a mental condition. Although this knowledge did not make my symptoms go away, it allowed me to be easier on myself when I repeatedly panicked because I had "lost" my keys again or when I started a task, wandered away and then could not remember what I was supposed to be doing or where I was supposed to be doing it.

Another aspect of "craziness" is magical thinking. Kübler-Ross's "Bargaining Stage" has a lot in common with the belief that if you think something hard enough, it will be so. Joan Didion wrote about the death of her husband in *The Year of Magical Thinking* (2006) and describes how nine months after her husband died, she could not get rid of his sneakers because she knew he would need them if he wanted to go running again. She continued to have this "crazy" thought, even though she had his ashes on a shelf in her living room.

I offer you this book because I have walked this path. I have lived through sudden widowhood, the challenges of continuing to raise the kids and see that they learned how to grow through catastrophe and continue with their own trajectories. I offer you some of my own stories to show you that you can get through this; the path back to wholeness is a hard road to travel but it can deepen your connections. It pares you down to your bones, to what is absolutely essential in your life. If the word "bereft" means to be deprived of some possession or of something intrinsic to you, the death of someone entwined in your life strips you of expectations and plans, as well as of your hopes and dreams for your future.

So now that it has happened to you, what can you do with it? Death has walked into the house of your life and left grief as a gift. Does that sound deranged? Grief is a gift?! This horrid morass of negativity, sorrow, anger, pity and disintegration? Let me explain, because I am *not* saying that the death of an important person in your life is the gift. No, that is the event that we are railing against, pounding our heads on the ground, moaning, "I did not want *this*." We mourn them, we miss them and we struggle through the assaults of this event on our psyches, emotions and even our physical selves.

The death of a loved one is so deep and so intense it is a life-changer. And this is where you might find the gift inside it. Finding yourself pared down to the core, as painful as it is, also takes you deep into the innermost parts of your Self. Here you might discover how you have changed by your association with the person who died. Up until the death, your definition of who you are has been defined by the relationship with this person; now, you have to figure out how to live without them. Your identity has been intertwined with theirs and now you have to figure out who you are, who you want to be. It's not going to be easy and it won't happen overnight. It will be intense and you may have times where you believe you cannot do it.

But if you are willing to take the challenge, you can discover ways to live again. As you move through the process of picking up the broken shards of life as you expected it to be, your reactions can begin to modulate. Slowly, as you cope with the pain and begin to consider how to live again, there might be opportunities for repair: to restore yourself, to rebuild and recreate a semblance of life. Cracking something open often reveals its essence. By considering your relationship, remembering good things and learning from the not-so-good things, you can heal to a certain extent. And if you allow yourself to feel all the emotions and discover your own skill and resilience, you can grow through this experience. And most importantly, you can carry your love for the person who died with you as you create your life on the other side of death.

The process of relearning how to live again after the devastating loss of someone so important not only shifts perspectives, it can actually be transformative. This idea of "opportunity" may seem odd, but that's my view. What other choice do we have, really?

I supposed we could choose to be bitter, to never laugh again, but that is not living. People do grieve in that way; we all know the example of Queen Victoria, who wore mourning black for 50 years after Prince Albert died. At the same time, she continued to reign, and found deep friendship with several retainers who offered her understanding and relief from her sorrow. In addition to her deep grief for Albert, to whom she erected monument after monument, she lived her life fully after his death. There are widows who choose never to date or marry again and create fulfilling, meaningful lives for themselves.

It is harder to accept grief as an opportunity when you have lost a child. If some of my words do not resonate with you because of the type of grief you are experiencing, know that you have my deepest sympathy. I cannot understand the depth of your particular loss, but I know how grief feels. I know it shifts over time and that no matter who has died in your life, how tragically or how wrongful their death was, you will find a way to live, somehow, again. You can find ways to feel more whole again, more complete even without this important person in your life in a physical way.

If there is something in this book that does not resonate with you, please just skip over it. I am a big one for making suggestions but I always offer them with the caveat that you don't have to try them if they don't feel right. Everyone is unique; your grief is your own and something might work or not. Maybe later, after some time has passed, you might investigate some idea you discarded and give it a try. Or not.

My story and why I wrote this book

I had been hearing a voice in my head periodically for about two years. I always pushed it aside, rationalized it away, told myself it was a silly message that made no sense.

It said:

"Death is stalking you."

This "voice" spoke in my ear every few months. It seemed so random and while I tried to ignore it, I also tried to figure out who it might be referring to. My elderly uncle? My mother-in-law? That made sense. I never considered that this intuitive sense was pointing to the person sleeping next to me. At the same time, it was clear that my husband was seriously stressed out. Several years before, his company in Boston had been purchased by a major Silicon Valley company in California and his work load had doubled. He was working so hard I thought it would kill him. He worked 12-hour, 15-hour, 18-hour days. He worked through the weekends. He was not sleeping well; he was eating too little. He was smoking too much. His company said they would pay for a vacation so he could re-group. We left before the kids woke up and I said, "Kiss them goodbye before we leave." "But they are sleeping," he answered. "No matter. Kiss them anyway," I insisted.

We went to New Mexico, a spiritual place for us. I wanted him to relax, totally. I wanted him to get back to himself. I decided we would do anything and nothing— whatever he wanted. My plan was to spend the first couple of days helping him be calm, helping him let go of all the stress from working so many hours for years on end. Our next plan was for Wednesday when we were scheduled to drive up to Ojo Caliente, the famous hot springs. We would soak, swab ourselves in mud, soak some more. We would have massages and then lunch. My plan was to begin to formulate a method for change in our lives. I wanted to say to him, "Let's change everything if that will help you to not work so hard. We can sell the house, we can move, I can get a full time job." I was hoping to start this conversation over dessert. Our other plan was to visit our old spiritual teacher, Elizabeth Cogburn, on Friday, which I hoped would help to solidify any changes we had agreed to on Wednesday.

Meanwhile, on Monday in Santa Fe, we walked, slept, went sight-seeing. We visited the Indian Market in the historic central plaza in Santa Fe, where he bought me a delicate silver and turquoise necklace. We sipped mint tea, our glasses brimming with fresh mint which we chewed after we sipped. We chatted with people at the next table as we ate lunch. We sat in the central plaza for a while because he was very tired. Turning around, we looked up to the mountains which were covered in snow. "I want to walk in the snow," he said, so we drove up above the snow line. I took pictures of him in his UConn tee shirt, balancing on a log across a stream.

> *He was happy but we couldn't breathe in the thin air.*
> *We laughed at ourselves and went down the mountain.*
> *We sat on a rooftop. We sipped Margaritas.*
> *We slept some more. I thought,*
> *my relaxation plan is working.*

~ (PERSONAL JOURNAL, OCTOBER 2006)

On Tuesday, a long-lost friend came to visit and we walked through art galleries, talking all day. We shared life stories, we told her about our marriage, our children, our travels, our joys and difficulties. We told her everything we had done in the past 20 years, complete with a small album of photos. After she left, we took a nap. Holding him gently as he slept, I could feel all the tension leave his body. "Good," I thought. My plan was working. He woke up and said he wanted to eat a hamburger, which was an unusual request for him. We looked in our guidebook and found a nearby place, called "Dave's Not Here." We ate, talked and laughed with each other.

Back in our hotel, we turned on the local news. I remember thinking that the newscasters looked very different than ours at home in New York—not quite as coiffed or polished. I left the room for a minute. When I returned, he was lying on the bed. He looked calm but suddenly, he gulped, a horrible, dry, gurgling sound emitted from his mouth. It was very loud.

> *He turned his head to the left.*
> *His face and his whole body turned dark blue.*
> *I grabbed him by his shoulders, shaking him.*
> *"Wait a minute. WAIT A MINUTE!!!*
> *Where are you going?"*
> *I screamed.*
>
> ~ (PERSONAL JOURNAL, OCTOBER 2006)

As I collapsed on the floor, I felt as if I was floating above the whole scene, I heard another voice in my head. It said:

> *"Your life has radically changed. Now what?"*

The people from the next room began CPR as soon as they responded to my screams. The proprietor of the bed and breakfast, which happened to be called "Casa Pacifica" or House of Peace, took turns until the EMTs arrived. It took them about 10 minutes to get there but the two people continued CPR until they took over. They tried valiantly for over an hour to revive him. It was clear from that last breath that this was not possible although I appreciated the attempt. The bed and breakfast proprietor got angry with them and started to complain loudly that they were too slow but I asked her to stop. I did not need her negativity when I could see how hard they were trying.

She gave me a different room to stay in, assuming that I would not want to be in the room in which he died. She was very wrong in this regard although it was a kind thought. I needed to stay in our room because I had an odd feeling that he was still there, floating somewhere above us, wondering why he was out of his body and why it was lying there, lifeless on the floor.

The couple from the next room asked if there was someone I could call. I called our friend Missy from Albuquerque with whom we had spent the day and she had someone drive her up to Santa Fe so that she could drive me where I needed to go. She wisely realized that I would be in no condition to drive anywhere, especially in a strange place.

I called Elizabeth, who answered by saying that she had been trying to call me since 9 pm. This was when he had taken his last breath. Apparently my phone could not receive calls once I dialed 911; someone figured this out and reset it for me. All I could say to her was, "He's dead. He's *dead*." She responded that she and her husband Robert would come to Santa Fe the next day.

The medics were ready to take him away. I asked for time to be with him alone. I asked if I could light candles and if I could light some sage to waft over him. The medical examiner gave me permission with the caveat that I make sure not to get any of the sage ash on his body. With our friend by my side, I touched his hair, kissed his face and told him how much I loved him, how precious our life together had been and how much I had grown because of him. I told him we would be alright and gave him permission to find peace in whatever realm he had entered, if there was one. I had so wanted him to relax and it seemed that he had relaxed so much that he had simply let go of this life. He, whose vigor had become so depleted by stress and overwork, had transformed into all energy.

Back at home in New York, the children were sleeping. Back at home in New York, my sister Jenny, Alby's sister Nancy, everyone in our family, were sleeping and they all needed to be notified. I needed to be the one to tell them, but the overarching problem was how to accomplish this from New Mexico. Alby's sister Nancy did not answer her phone, so I was forced to call Jenny and her husband Bill and ask them, in the midst of their own sorrow and shock, to drive to Nancy's house and pound on her door. I could hear my sister screaming in the background while I came up with a plan with my brother-in-law Bill. We decided that they, along with Nancy and her husband Dan, would go to my house at 6 am to be with the children. Once they were there, I would call to break the news.

Over and over throughout the night, I called people, woke them up, listened to them scream and told them that Alby was dead. Word began to spread and by morning friends began calling to ask if it was true. I called Alby's office to tell them, and his colleague Stuart went immediately to my house to be with the children. When the corporate office called me, I flatly told them that they had killed him.

At 4 am New Mexico time, my sister called to say that they were at the top of our street. I waited a few minutes, perhaps a minute too long, because when my daughter opened the door and saw the long, shocked faces of her aunts and uncles, she immediately knew something bad had happened. She blurted out, "Is it Daddy?" Chloë, Eben and Ilana were already in tears when I called, even though they did not know exactly what had happened.

For the next two days, until I boarded the plane to return home, I made sure there was adequate support for the kids at home, whether it was an aunt or uncle or a close family friend. The mother of one of my daughter's friends called the school to explain why they were not coming in and specifically asked that the staff be told but that no announcement be made. This did not prevent the music teacher informing the 200 students in the band, first thing in the morning, that Ilana and Eben's father had died. Now my own phone and our home phone were flooded with calls, and some people even drove over to our house. I fielded calls from my sister-in-law, asking her to be the gatekeeper, authorizing her to request that people leave since I was not yet home.

Elizabeth and Robert Cogburn came to see me the next day. I was in a fog; they sat with me making gentle conversation until I was more settled. Elizabeth suggested a walk by the Rio Grande River, which was a tiny trickle of a stream in the middle of Santa Fe. Like an automaton, I followed her, walking among the stones and large green leaves, wondering where the water was, wondering where I was. When we returned to the Casa Pacifica, Elizabeth asked me what I needed.

I told Elizabeth that I was afraid Alby was floating up by the ceiling and if I left, he would be stuck in New Mexico.

I knew this was not a rational thought but I imagined him hovering there, about a foot below the ceiling with a very concerned expression on his face. Elizabeth led us in a guided meditation designed to talk with Alby, and in my heart I told him I loved him and that he could leave. She lit sage and sent the smoke into all the corners of the room at the Casa Pacifica. Missy went to the car and turned it on, taking my suitcases with her. Elizabeth shooed me out, wafting smoke behind me as if she were wafting his spirit along with me. "Don't stop," she said, and I got into the car and we drove away. She continued to send the smoke in my direction. We drove off to Albuquerque.

I woke up at 3 am, feeling as if he were lying in the bed next to me, a phenomenon so real that I could sense his weight on the bed, feel his body snuggling against mine. Rubbing the air as if I were caressing him, I said, "You have to come with me. We have to go back to the children."

Despite my angry accusation to the person who called from his corporation, they treated me with kindness. They arranged for me to fly first class and organized the transport of his body back to New York after the autopsy was complete. They arranged for a limo to drive me home, and my sisters came to the airport to wait for me, bringing my oldest daughter along so that I would not have to ride alone. The airline told me that they would not leave me alone when I transferred planes but this turned out to be untrue since I did not need a wheelchair, only someone to walk with me. I solved this problem by calling Eben and talking with him the whole time I walked through the airport and rode a tram to a different terminal. Since our car was parked at a different airport, our friend Stuart picked up the keys and drove the two hours with another friend so that he could retrieve Alby's car.

During the next couple of weeks, friends and family surrounded us. I called in people from the past and from the present and wrote a ceremony, assisted by Darrah Cloud, playwright and close friend. Alby's best friend Adam arrived from California, my friends arrived from far and near. My sisters made sure that we ate. Adam kept handing me a citrus-y fizzy drink, which I found out later contained Vitamin C and electrolytes. My sister-in-law Mandy, whose family was from Hawaii, had orchid leis shipped in for us to wear at his memorial celebration. Nancy and Alby's brother Chris arranged for a wake, which their side of the family needed.

My catering staff took over the logistics of our Celebration of Life for Alby. Nancy's spacious backyard contained a large tent, and Lori and Alice arranged food and beverages for a crowd. The ceremony spoke to different aspects of his life, from our earliest work with Elizabeth to commemorations written by each of the children and one by me. Adam and Eben made a soundtrack of Alby's favorite music and the tent was filled with urns of lilacs, framed photographs and two ee cummings poems that were meaningful to our lives together. Nancy set up a spiral-shaped path in her back garden, near some apple trees. My friend Darrah donated a large granite bowl which Nancy filled with river stones and placed at the center of the path. Mourners were invited to visit this path, walk slowly in a spiral and take a stone from the bowl in memory of Alby. He would have loved that.

Dangling your feet on the edge of the abyss

People are afraid of overwhelming, devastating emotions. Many of my clients have observed that they are afraid to express these feelings, because they fear they will plunge into a hole that they will not be able to get out of. This metaphorical abyss looms in front of them. My suggestion is to sit down at the edge, dangling your feet, while considering what to do. This "rest" before the plunge also demonstrates ways to care for yourself while you are grieving.

Death opens up a hole in your life and you might feel as if you are teetering on the edge of it. It is challenging to allow yourself to give in to strong emotion, to metaphorically fall into the abyss. What will happen to you in there? How will you manage to lift yourself out of this darkness? This trepidation causes a desire to suppress emotion, to not "give in" to sadness. Many share this statement: "I am afraid that if I start crying, I won't be able to stop." Indeed, the feeling of falling apart that accompanies deep sorrow can be very frightening, especially when you already feel broken. In addition, the idea that one must be strong in the face of disaster causes many to put on a stoic front. Others fear they will burden their family and friends by expressing their deepest feelings. And so, we stand shakily at the edge, overwhelmed and filled with dread.

The Merriam-Webster dictionary defines abyss as an "immeasurably deep gulf or space" or "the bottomless gulf, pit or chaos of the old cosmogonies." The word "cosmogony" refers to a theory of the creation of the world or universe. In other words, the abyss that opens up after death is a huge, seemingly bottomless rift in our understanding of our world. This black hole teems with emotions such as fear, insecurity, yearning, desperation, gloom and misery. It is not a pretty metaphor; in fact it often feels quite frightening. So it is no wonder that you may worry that if you accidentally fall in, you might never get out.

The other side of this thought is that while you may postpone plunging in to all the crazy emotions, ultimately they cannot be avoided. They are too strong. Suppressed emotions will undoubtedly come back and bite you when you least expect them to. So what is the solution for coping with this dark expanse?

My recommendation is to have a seat, right there on the edge of the abyss. If you like, you can tuck your feet underneath you but if you are very brave (or willing to be vulnerable) you can dangle your feet into the black hole. It's okay. You are safe on the edge right now. Take a deep breath. Rest here on the brink of the unknown. This darkness below you, stretching out in front of you, is the vast, empty terrain of loss. It is frightening, yet you can take your time. You don't have to enter until you are ready. You don't have to handle it all at once, either. You can dip a toe in, sense how much you can stand, then pull back. Take your time. Try to enter the abyss in increments, dosing yourself then sitting back down right there, at the edge.

But ultimately, there is no turning back. You cannot return to your old life; it is changed now. Yes, you may fear you don't have the ability to handle this. Yes, perhaps you are afraid you will drown in that murk.

You won't drown, especially since you are just sitting on the verge of entering, observing this abyss. It is not really there anyway; it is a metaphor, a perception of the rupture in your life. By sitting on the edge of it, you can breathe. Gather your resources. What tools do you need to help you? Do you need a metaphorical life-preserver? What would it look like? Can you bring along a symbolic rope to help pull yourself out? Can you remind yourself, as you tip tentatively over the edge, that this dark, seemingly bottomless hole has been created not only by death but also by love?

We cannot mourn what we did not love. We do not grieve over someone we don't care about. Our memories and shared history with that person can become our raft. Our love becomes buoyancy which will enable us to float to the surface, once we have spent some time within the darkness. Remember that darkness and the seemingly negative side of things are not necessarily bad. Mammals all gestate in the dark fluid space of the womb. Ideas and thoughts find form in the dark recesses of our minds, incubating like seeds in dark soil before the spring. Embrace the dark for it can be nurturing. Enter the abyss with the knowledge that your love will carry you through.

The bottomless gulf that has swallowed up the shards of life as you knew it also offers the tools for repair. Allowing yourself some time for emotional release, while recognizing its connection to love, opens you up to the possibilities of discovering what your new world might look like. Rising back up to the surface after your plunge into the dark depths demonstrates your own resilience and highlights your ability to survive grief's pain.

It is going to take time, perhaps longer than you think. Certainly it will take longer than other people think it should, so be prepared for "helpful" suggestions that you should be done with it at any certain date. The abyss of loss is a fearsome "place" but slowly, you will discover your own inner abilities which will help you swim across to the other side of your own life.

When we enter into an alien territory such as the strange landscape of life after loss, we long for clear guidance. We question our every reaction and worry that we are not "grieving correctly." Unfortunately, outsiders don't know how to help us and what little they know about grief processing is usually wrong. On top of that, even people who care about us in our bereaved state are at a loss; they are not sure what to say or how to help. Our sad, pale faces, our sometimes vacant stares and the heaviness that emanates from our bodies can be extremely troubling for friends and family who wish they could find just the right phrase of comfort that would make us feel better, that would "fix" us.

A man came to my office one month after his wife died in a terrible accident. Tears rolled down his cheeks as he asked for guidance, saying, "I don't think I am doing this right." He was surrounded by close, caring friends who were very worried about him since he was normally a happy-go-lucky person. Now he was crying all the time, walking around in a fog. His friends tried to think of ways to help him feel better. One told him that he would feel better if he just took off his wedding ring. Another told him to go fishing and another suggested that he clear out all her clothes because they "reminded" him of his wife.

These suggestions come from a well-meaning place but they also come from people who do not quite understand. Out of their love for their grieving friend, they were attempting to help by offering ideas they hoped might "fix" a situation which is actually unfixable. Some of these statements might even contain an idea that is comforting, but most of them feel jarring to him, making him angry. For example, the idea of removing his wedding ring was so horrific to the man in my office that he physically cringed when he told me about it. He was also so early in his grief that he wondered if perhaps his friend was right. He did not want to take off his ring but he also did not want to feel so bad.

Elisabeth Kübler-Ross, the grandmother of research into death, dying and bereavement, originally published her research on the Stages of Dying. These were created after observing and listening to hundreds of dying patients and identifying common themes. Prior to her research, people did not talk to the dying, did not even tell them how ill they were or share the knowledge of their terminality with them. Kübler-Ross did something other doctors had not thought of; she talked with terminally ill patients, asking them how they felt, what they thought was happening to them and what they needed. Her research confirmed that dying patients were often acutely aware of their own impending death, and the secrecy did not help either the patient or the family. Her pioneering work opened discussions and brought honesty and compassion to the deathbed. She also turned her focus to family members and found that by talking openly, it was sometimes easier for them to grieve after their loved one died. The five stages were based on common feelings she observed in the dying, which also appeared to be present in the experiences of many of the bereaved. Kübler-Ross eventually applied her stages to bereavement and now, her Stages of Grief are commonly known and unfortunately nearly always misunderstood. Because her theory and model of grief is in book form, presenting these stages in chapters, it appears that there is a linear way to move through the process. One reads the book from beginning to end and assumes that this is a prescription for grief.

While Kübler-Ross's work was ground-breaking, the misapplication of her stages has created the erroneous idea that one *must* go through particular stages or else one is not grieving correctly. There is also a false notion that your grief can be resolved through these five stages and if you are still feeling sad after a certain, usually short, period of time, you must have skipped a stage. In reality, Kübler-Ross is quite clear in all her books that there is no right way to grieve; that one might experience some or all of her "stages" and one might even go through them in a different order or be in several stages at the same time.

The good news is that Kübler-Ross radically changed our culture's approach to death, making it acceptable to talk about it. The problem is that the Stages of Grief have entered popular culture, skipping the important clarification that grief is not linear and no one grieves in the same way. The stages are mentioned on TV shows and in movies. Medical professionals, who rarely study anything about death, dying and bereavement, latch on to some version of the five stages and think this is "how" we are supposed to grieve. Even well-meaning therapists, if they have not studied thanatology or are not conversant in current research into bereavement, have an expectation that their grieving clients will start with denial, spend a day or two bargaining, express some anger, feel a bit depressed and then, BOOM! Acceptance. And, we're done.

It is too bad for Kübler-Ross, because now that she has been so simplified and misunderstood, she is also derided by the bereavement research community. This is unfortunate because her observations still have merit if we could loosen up our view of them as a rigid, linear paradigm and remember that she never meant them to be so. At the same time, in the 30-plus years since Kübler-Ross, thanatologists have been conducting research studies, developing new models that are more open and aligned with how people grieve. These newer models are clearer and more flexible than the five stages. Do bereaved people feel anger, depression and go through a process of acceptance than includes some denial in the beginning? Of course many do. But there is no one way to grieve.

In her own words, Kübler-Ross says this:

The stages have evolved since their introduction, and they have been very misunderstood over the past three decades. They were never meant to help tuck messy emotions into neat packages. They are responses to loss that many people have, but there is not a typical response to loss as there is no typical loss. Our grieving is an individual as our lives.

The five stages…are a part of the framework that makes up our learning to live with the one we lost. They are tools to help us frame and identify what we may be feeling. But they are not stops on some linear timeline in grief. Not everyone goes through all of them or goes through them in a prescribed order. (Kübler-Ross and Kessler, 2005, p.7)

In fact, it is possible to experience a couple of these "stages" at the same time, such as feeling depressed and angry all at once. You may find that you are moving through in a way that feels like a straight line, as if you are "making progress," stabilizing and not feeling quite as raw or as sad all the time. You may breathe a sigh of relief only to discover that the next day, you are plunged back into despair, extreme emotional upheaval and confusion. This is how it goes. Up, down, backwards and forwards, sideways even.

I want to make you a promise. I promise you can do this. I promise that you will get through this and find a way to feel calmer, perhaps even content again. I promise that, with time and energy, with exploration and support, you will survive. This book is designed to help you do just that—but it is up to you. Meanwhile:

- Don't let anyone tell you that you are not grieving correctly.

- Don't let anyone tell you what you *should* be feeling. Even yourself.

- Don't tell yourself you "should" be grieving in any other way than how you are.

Your grief is unique to you. You might indeed feel angry, you may find yourself bargaining or you might have difficulty accepting this death, which is sometimes referred to as denial. I feel that most of my clients who are "in denial" are really going through the necessary adjustment to life after death. Accepting the death and what it means to your life is a many-layered process. For instance, even though you rationally know that the person has died, you may have trouble actually believing it. You might have dreams in which the person is alive and well. You might have flashbacks, reliving those last moments over and over. If you were not present at their death, you may have flashbacks to how you found out or you might have dreams that are filled with horrible imaginings of what may have happened. You might wake in the morning and reach for them, then shockingly remember that they are gone. Slowly, over time, this shock wears off. Denial would be claiming that they are not dead and will walk through the door any minute.

How to use this book

The simple answer to the question of how to use this book is "any way you wish." Grief is not a linear experience and any attempt at learning to cope with it is also not linear. In fact, this is one of the many difficult things about the experience. It is a crazy, mixed-up, back and forth, rolling and sliding type of thing. Therefore, even though this book is built upon the word "WHOLE," breaking it into an acronym, there is no requirement that you follow through it in that order.

Feel free to move around this book, rather than reading it from cover to cover. A book is organized from beginning to end, seeming to guide you in a straight line, but the process of healing after death is anything but. Grief is a spiral, a slogging stopping and rushing forward, filled with crazy highs and dark lows. The WHOLE process is organized in a linear way because it is a metaphor. You may find that the most compelling part for you is Chapter 3 on "How can I get through this?" For you to become whole again through your grief process, you may find that reviewing your relationship (exploring the past) is important to take on early. Even though this appears to be the last part of the WHOLE process, it really was one of the first things I did in the early months of grief.

Throughout the book, there are suggestions for activities and exercises for you to try. These are offered because I have done them, many of my clients have engaged with them and they might work for you. Some of them are designed to help you process grief in a journal, others are ways to express your grief creatively. Often mere words are not enough to capture and release all the emotions we feel when we are grieving, therefore using color, imagination, imagery and other forms of expression can really help. I invite you to experiment with these even if you don't think of yourself as particularly "creative." Give yourself permission to give voice to your inner world as you navigate through it.

I'd like to give you permission to grieve in your own unique way, explore your pain and sorrow and any other emotions that arise, with love and gentleness as you move along the path of your life now that your loved one has died. I hope this book is helpful to you.

The WHOLE process

For me, the quest for wholeness was an overarching concern, almost as important as my desire to be free from the agony of loss. I intrinsically knew that the only way to get past the pain was to go through it, and being the kind of proactive, fearless or perhaps naïve person that I am, I decided the best course of action was to plunge into the deep end of my sorrow. I did this without holding my nose; I did this without being able to see the bottom of the pit of despair that I was careening into. Yet I knew that I would manage. I am not a person who is afraid of the dark, whether it is actual night or the darkest night of my very soul. I bravely entered the depths of my life, of my sadness and anger, of my abandonment and the catastrophe that colored my days. While I was being so brave, I was also terrified, anxious, and was fairly certain that something else really bad would happen. I did not know any other widows my age. I moved through the world like a deer caught in the headlights and imagined there was a neon sign just above my forehead that flashed two words alternating in orange light:

- "WIDOW"

- "TRAGEDY"

Picking up the pieces of myself to become whole again was imperative, even though I had no idea what shape my life would take. I only knew that he was dead, irrevocably dead. And I was alive and I had to figure out how to live again.

So I am using this word "WHOLE" to describe a way to get through your own grief.

This "method," if you will, allows you to navigate the morass in spurts, parsing aspects of the process and coping with it, bit by bit. The concept of a journey implies a relatively straight path, but this one winds around, doubling back on itself or taking you sideways. I actually believe that the twists and turns of processing tragic and difficult events in one's life is the whole point of it all. In other words, the movement itself leads towards healing, if that is at all possible. You will be changed by this experience and you may even stimulate some growth as you knit yourself and your life back together again. This view might be a more reasonable one than any idea of "closure," because closure implies an ending of something. Our grief will never totally end although it will shift as we digest it. There is no real completion after death. You are not going to get through a process, whether it is the five stages, the four tasks, reconstructing your life or relearning your world—you are not going to wake up one morning and think, "Okay, I am *done* with grief." If we can accept that this is not possible, might we accept the challenge of experience and be willing to shift with it? After all, as much as we wish it not to be so, life is all about change. Now that your life has radically changed, what *is* next?

The common misconception about loss is that we will one day be "ourselves" again, as we were before they died. Sigmund Freud thought that's how it worked and wrote a paper on it in 1917 in which he said that we must "decathect" or withdraw our feelings of attachment from the object of our love and then we can get on with our lives.

Freud had a lot of interesting ideas and changed the way the world thinks, philosophically and psychologically, but this suggestion that you might never think about your darling or your dear father or sister again is, well, ridiculous.

No. The process of coming back to wholeness includes figuring out a way to continue the bond with this person who has died. In the thanatology world, this is called just that: "continuing bonds." Psychologist William Worden (2009) felt that the word "stages" implied something passive in that we pass through them, whereas grief is more active. Through his research, he developed a model for working through grief and identified four tasks of mourning as necessary parts of the grieving process. Worden's Model begins with accepting the loss, feeling the pain associated with it, adjusting to life afterwards and discovering ways to continue to remain connected to the person who has died. I sum up Worden's tasks by saying we learn to Accept, Feel, Adjust and Continue.

Worden points out that no one is required to go through these tasks in "a fixed progression and fall into the trap associated with fixed stages. Tasks can be revisited and worked through again and again over time. Various tasks can also be worked on *at the same time*. Grieving is a fluid process..." (Worden, 2009, p.53).

I like that last statement. If we think of our grief as fluid, it is entirely possible that we won't get stuck in it. If it is fluid, we can experience its upheavals as ebb and flow, even if we resist it at times.

Another cliché often repeated is "Time heals all wounds." Will time heal these wounds? Will you one day wake up and feel no sadness, no longer wish they were still alive and sharing life with you? Probably not. Does time affect your reactions? Over the long term, yes. One gentleman in a support group said, "My grief does not ever really go away but it softens with time." This refers to the stark rawness of its early part, that sharp stab of realization that keeps catching you when you least expect it. Slowly, over time, the pain becomes less agonizing. Slowly, over time, your extreme reactions temper.

Nonetheless, the idea that you will someday feel better does not ring true in the beginning. One month after my husband died, I wrote this:

> *My heart is broken.*
> *all my love, all my focus*
> *my intention, my attention*
> *is suspended.*
> *I move through the world*
> *cleaning up your messes*
> *doing your chores, making dinner*
> *starting a new quilt.*
> *What for.*
> *Why.*
> *Why did you*
> *leave me?*

~ (PERSONAL JOURNAL, JUNE 2005)

The problem with the idea of time and its supposed healing properties is that you cannot imagine a future when someone dies. They have been such an integral part of your life that you have trouble picturing your life without them.

It seems as if all hopes, dreams and plans are also shattered before you.

In reality, there is no one way to "process" loss. You are going to have a difficult time no matter what you do, no matter how hard you try not to grieve or how much you allow yourself to express your feelings. But there are some clear models, some theories, a whole lot of research and several methods that can help you. Please, try them on for size. Try what I am offering you; it may be helpful. Please remember, though, that even as this process of discovering your wholeness is presented here by using the initials of the word WHOLE in order, there is absolutely no reason why you cannot start with Chapter 6 or Chapter 3. Skim through this process and see what feels right to you, at this time. Explore your grief as if it were an interesting landscape that has something, some quality, that ultimately will shift your life. Because, as strange as that sounds, in many ways it will. You will never completely "get over" this loss of this person, so integral to your life. But the things you have learned through being in relationship with them and the way this relationship has affected you will continue. Grief, the process of mourning and of slowly putting yourself and your life back together will alter you. Some of these changes will simply be, well, somewhat different than before. And some of these modifications might even bring forward thoughts, passions, ideas that your loved one would have wanted to do, complete, or be involved with. No matter what, you probably will be a different person on the other side of this experience. It might help to be proactive about it, to make some conscious choices along the way.

CHAPTER 2

W

What Happened? Who Am I?

We need to tell our stories in order to understand what happened. This chapter explores the importance of our personal narratives.

There are many ways to tell the story of your loss. By telling it in different ways, it can be transformed. Storytelling becomes the pathway to reworking some aspects of the story that are uncomfortable. Storytelling can help soothe difficult emotions and heal sticky relationships with other people who might be grieving the same death but in a different way.

Telling your story to others helps you grapple with the reality of it. Working with your own narrative explains the events to yourself, exposes and perhaps clears up misunderstandings and develops insights into what happened. There may be unanswerable questions so reviewing the narrative, and retelling your story in different ways helps you develop a story you can live with when the one you keep repeating is no longer serving you.

You must tell your story 72 times in order to heal

Honestly, I have no idea where I read this phrase but it continued to ring in my head ever since I found it, several months into my own loss. It rang true because I was telling the story of his death over and over, to anyone who would listen (and to some who would not or who had heard it several times already). The story of what happened those last few days was so strange, so shocking and out of sync with what was "supposed" to be that I kept telling it. Again and again. When I read this adage, I thought that for me, given the sudden nature of his death, I needed to tell the story 72 times just to believe it.

But our stories are important for many reasons. As you tell the story, it begins to happen, and perhaps this is why we feel compelled to tell and retell our important event stories. The reality begins to settle as we tell it.

For months after he died, I found myself telling this story. Every detail was imprinted in my brain, but my heart was unable to believe it. That shocking moment when I grabbed him, the dusky blue color of his face, the unreality of the moments that followed. I did not often repeat the part where I banged on the adjoining door to the next room, trying to get someone to help me. I did not tell

people over and over how I did not know the address of
the bed and breakfast, so that when the 911 operator asked
me, I stammered and handed my phone to someone else.
Or how I hyperventilated after he died and had to be given
oxygen. I kept telling the story again and again as if it were
the only way I could believe it.

At around eight months after Alby's death, someone
asked me what had happened. As I launched into my story, I
listened to myself and recognized that it had become a well-
rehearsed, honed tale. The words I used were nearly the
same every time. It had lost its emotional power and had
become a sort of parable. I recognized it was time to tell a
different story. I began to tell the story of our lives together
and of what a good man he was, before I told the part of his
untimely end. I began to tell the story of relationship and
of our growth, of our family and of our children. I began to
tell the story of our life rather than the story of his death.

There are so many ways to tell the important stories of
our lives. There is the story of what happened, of course:
the facts and nothing but the facts, which tends to get a little
stale after a while. What if we could explore our stories
from different angles?

If I told my story from an emotional perspective, I
would tell it like this:

For many years, Alby had been working too hard. At first
I was resentful because our ability to co-parent our growing
family was impacted. He was hardly ever home and I felt
abandoned by this. When I was caught up in my own hurt
feelings, I did not easily see that he was hurting as well. He
felt cut off from his family, and the pressure to do well in his
changed work environment was also a pressure to do well

for his family. And as he worked longer and longer hours to support us, I felt less and less supported.

Sometime in his last two years it slowly dawned on me that he was so stressed, he was in danger. Not only was he in physical danger because he was not eating properly but I also felt that he had lost touch with his core, the essence of his being, his spiritual center. When we decided to go away, I felt like this trip would save his soul. I felt as if it was a desperate last chance to reconnect both with our inner selves and with each other.

He was so exhausted and depleted. When we lay down on that last day to take a nap, I held him close. I felt him completely relax and I thought, "Here we go. Now we can change things and he will regain his energy." A few hours later, he took that last shuddering breath and became all energy, leaving his blue body lying there on the bed, in the Casa Pacifica in Santa Fe.

I can also tell my story from the perspective of our relationship, telling you how when I first saw him my heart dropped. I can tell you how we became close friends before we became lovers and how he slowed me down as much as I stimulated him to embrace a slightly faster path to marriage and children. He taught me about unconditional love by giving 100 percent of his heart. Our relationship was grounded in a deep quest for connection; indeed, one of our earliest "vacations" was a two-week gathering in the Jemez Mountains, where we considered how to keep the bubbles in the champagne of long-term relationship. While we had some difficult times, we always remembered to reconnect, to enjoy each other's gifts.

We explain who we are by the narratives we tell. Our stories become an expression of who we think we are, so it behooves us to pay attention. At grief's beginning, telling the story of what happened seems imperative and enables us to understand what happened. Telling the story again and again allows us to investigate it, to work through the "What?" and "Why?" of it. As we begin to explore it, how we tell our story deepens as we consider the impact of this huge change on our lives. Slowly, we begin to recognize different sides of our own narrative. We move from emotional reactions to a review of the relationship, allowing us to consider what we learned from this person and how our lives changed in knowing them. Telling the story in this way can help reconcile aspects of the relationship and discover its meaning.

Considering the story from a mythic perspective allows us to honor the impact it had. Perhaps you were a caregiver to your loved one when they were ill and dying. The focus, vigilance and love you provided could be viewed as heroic. If you were to tell your story, casting yourself as its hero, how would it change the way you perceive what happened? The mythic story can also be the story of the tribulations you encounter along the way, since coping with it is so hard. This is a journey that has no maps, no landmarks, and often the journey feels as if it has no destination. Traveling the paths of grief can be seen as moving away from your loved one but it is actually a spiraling path into your own center. Would it be helpful to view it as a quest?

Just as the death of someone close changes our lives, sometimes radically, the process itself could be transformative in certain ways. Developing new narratives helps us subtly begin to discover new aspects to our own stories. How will this experience of grief change you? As you begin to adapt to life without this person, what shape will your life take? Can your sorrow and anguish stimulate you to see your life in a different way? When you get to the other side of raw emotion, when you crafted meaningful stories of the events and aspects of your relationship, will you be able to grow through this crucible of pain? How you tell your story can help you discover the possibility of a transformed life, one that is rich, full and happy even though your loved one is no longer physically in it. Over time, you can slowly learn to live again, not in spite of their death but because of it.

phase two
look at all the pieces
keep what fits together
discard what is
unnecessary
Rebuild
design a new story
and make it a good one
a magical one.

~ (PERSONAL JOURNAL, NOVEMBER 2005)

Tell your story

Thinking about the person who has died, what story do you need to tell? Reflect on this for a few minutes then write your story in your journal or on a pad of paper. Enrich it with details: who was there, what they did or said. Include what you did and how you felt.

Your story is important. Write it down in all its facets. Keep it for yourself, or share it with others (but only if you want to).

How do you tell your story? Are you caught up in describing the events surrounding the death? Who was present at the time and what did they say or do? Who was there to help you when you found out, if you were not present at the time?

Often after someone dies, as we wish that it had never happened, we spend some time imagining that we could have prevented it in some way. We might even be angry at doctors or the other driver or the disease or the weather, whatever we perceive as the cause of the death. This is a normal reaction. I call these the "What Ifs" or the "If Onlys." They can hijack our thoughts and while they seem to interfere with grief, they are actually a natural part of it. The "What Ifs" demand answers, and rather than telling ourselves a story about how silly these thoughts are, we could allow them to have a voice for a little while before subjecting them to some reality testing.

I had a client who spent many sessions going over and over what she could have done to prevent her father's death. If only she had taken him for a third opinion. If only she had managed to get him on the transplant list. Her regret and self-blame, her hyped-up sense of personal responsibility for his life, reflected her loss but it also reflected the potential losses coming up. She had been unable to carry a baby to term and had a miscarriage shortly before he died. Now he would never know her child should she have one. Her repeated attempts to blame herself (if only she had done something, she would have been his savior) did not take into account the fact that her mother and her father made specific decisions regarding his treatment and had consulted several different doctors for their opinions. Her parents had come to a conscious conclusion that no treatment of his cancer would reverse it and had accepted that he was dying. Since she did not want to lose her father, she pinned her hopes on the possibility of one more doctor who might come up with a different opinion or perhaps a miracle. After he died, she continued to ask the "What If" questions.

In counseling sessions, we explored each of her "What If" scenarios. I encouraged her to explore her feelings about his death and her sorrow over the fact that she had not produced a grandchild while he was alive.

Once my client acknowledged the root cause of her regret, which was more about her own childless state and her disappointment in that arena, she was able to stop the If Onlys and focus more on her sadness over her father's death and her longing for his presence. She was able to tell a different story, one in which she expressed her continued love for him. She was able to tell a different story about her life—not one of regret but one of hope. A year later she gave birth to a daughter and named her after her father.

Often, family members have different reactions to the death of the same person. For example, in the case of the death of a parent, one child may feel that they took on more responsibility for the care of the parent than other siblings. This is often true and, anyway, it is true in their perception. After the death of the parent, I have listened to complaints about other siblings who did not visit, did not make decisions and who even criticized the one who did make choices on behalf of the parent. Habits of behavior that have their roots in the family structure play out after the death.

In one case, an elderly woman died in a hospice, leaving behind two adult daughters. Their father had died many years before and the mother was a combination of a strong and dependent woman, with a habit of complaining about one daughter to the other. She made herself the lynchpin between the daughters, who always talked to her before they talked to each other. The older daughter was married and had two grown children with a few grandchildren. The younger daughter, my client, was a successful career woman who did not marry until she was 60 years old. Since she had no children, she did many things with her nieces and their children but she always felt that she had to ask her sister's permission before she took them to the ballet or the movies, even before she called them on the phone. She longed to do things with her sister but was not particularly fond of her sister's husband, partially because it seemed to her that he often made decisions for his wife.

As an outside witness to these patterns of behavior, it occurred to me that this was a habit of triangulation set by the mother. I asked my client if the way she and her sister related to each other reminded her of anyone else. She replied, "My mother!" Still, she spent several counseling sessions complaining about her sister and how she wished she was able to have a better relationship with her.

Why?

Curiosity is a trait that helps us investigate our world. I have always been curious, about the way things work, about meanings and about connections and synchronicities. I have always asked "Why?" as if knowing the answer to this vast question could solve everything.

When you are a kid, asking "Why?" is the way you learn. My Opa was always ready with an explanation if I asked why it snowed or why their neighbor Mrs. Coleman always closed her eyes and tipped her head back when she spoke. He did not have a satisfactory answer for this one but discussed the possibilities nevertheless. This taught me a greater truth: Sometimes the question "Why?" might not have a clear answer or may even have several potential answers.

"Why?" seems like an important question after a death. Why did it happen? Why me? Why him? Why couldn't it be prevented? Why did she have one more drink? Why did he drive down that road, at that rate of speed? Why didn't the doctors diagnose, treat, cure or do whatever it takes to stop this death? The "Whys" often get turned inward as we self-inflict with guilt, worry and second-guessing. Why didn't I see this coming? Why didn't I take him for that second or third opinion, get her on the transplant list/to a therapist/in a safer car? Why did we need milk that stormy night?

The "Why" question has been such a recurring one for me that once, when I was told by a teacher that I needed to stop asking so many questions, I immediately asked, "Why?" But I have slowly come to understand that often why something happened is unanswerable. When this realization dawned on me, it shifted the question from "Why?" to a consideration: Can I live with not knowing? Can I accept that the answer might always be mysterious and indecipherable?

Part of the "Why" question is also an attempt to see if there were some other choices that could have been made, some other path that could have been taken that would have not resulted in death.

In a way, there always are other paths and other possibilities that could have been taken, except that they were not. I had a client who was diagnosed with mesothelioma in his 50s and died several months later. His family spent a lot of time wondering why; trying to figure out where he might have been exposed to asbestos or other substances which caused his cancer and his early demise. Was it possible that if he had not had that one job out of many, he would not have been exposed and then he would not have had cancer and then he would not be dead? Of course it is possible and the family spent a considerable amount of mental and emotional energy on thoughts like these. I can't say that these thoughts were a waste of time because they helped the family realize that for all their trying to find out why he developed this cancer, the fact was that he did. He had it and he died from it. At a certain point, "Why?" stops being so important. Asking this question over and over is really an attempt to hold the sorrow at bay. Like anger, "Why?" keeps us from feeling what is threatening to drown us—wave upon wave of sadness. You might find this advice for answering children helpful:

> "Why?" The attempt to understand is fruitless, because no amount of understanding will dull the pain. When children ask you the "why?" you have asked yourself a thousand times, know they are not just looking for an answer, because no answer will ever be good enough. They are looking for ways to get rid of the pain, to make the sorrow go away, lift the grayness in their lives. Death is illogical and often senseless. You can't reason the pain away.
>
> Nor can you rush through this passage or deny it its due. The sorrow needs to be expressed. Sometimes it is spoken through art or poetry or dance or running wildly through the woods. Sometimes it is just there in the silence at the breakfast table. (Coloroso, 2000, p.33)

With Alby, I spent some time within the questioning space of "Why?" Why didn't he go to the doctor when he was feeling so unwell those last couple of years? Why didn't he say no when his job demanded more and more hours and he got less and less sleep, less and less food or time to relax, and hardly any time with his family? After a while, I turned my thoughts away from "Why?" and tried to focus on what *is*. I needed to accept the reality of his death and to understand that there was nothing I could do to change it. Ruminating on what had not been done, for whatever reason, was ultimately not going to benefit my process of grief.

"Karma," he said

On the first anniversary of Alby's death, a friend launched into a story of his neighbor who had been complaining about how he kept his yard. A wind storm arose and a tree fell across this neighbor's front steps. My friend ended his story with a loud, "Karma!" indicating that he thought the tree was some kind of cosmic retribution of the neighbor's bad behavior.

Sometimes this word gets tossed around to explain "Why?" I admit spending a little time after hearing this story, thinking/wondering why it was my "karma" to be suddenly widowed. Did I cause his death in some way? Had I been a "bad person" who was now reaping the cause of my past behavior? I quickly saw that this line of thinking was really useless, sort of like a child's magical thinking. Under closer examination, it appears that any possible rules of cause and affect apply at times, and at others, not so much. Our attempts to understand the working of the world, why human interactions generate certain causes or certain effects can send us spinning down a rabbit hole with no end in sight.

Karma is a concept with real meaning in Buddhism and Hinduism and it is not the same thing as a boomerang in which I yell at you and you yell at me and that's my "karma" coming back to me. I cannot attempt to explain deeply held religious beliefs in which I am not trained nor will I try to explain the unexplainable, but consider this: It is as if I were trying to hold the wind in my hand and then blamed myself for not having a good enough grasp. We do not know why someone lives or why someone dies. We can spend time trying to explain it to ourselves but, in the end, we do not know and we cannot change it.

Why is this happening to me?

But I want to know WHY
Why did he stop living
Why did he come to this place and float off
Why did he leave me?
Why did he leave us alone?

~ (PERSONAL JOURNAL, JULY 2005)

P was a woman in her 50s who lived with her long-term partner in the home in which she grew up. She was the second child of five, although she functioned as if she were the oldest. Her older sister was a recent widow, living about a half hour away. The family was Irish Catholic and their father was a veteran of World War II. P had been very close to her mother, who had died a long, slow death of cancer about 16 years before. P felt that she had never really recovered from the loss of her mother. Her father had been in a nursing home for a while, due to alcohol-induced dementia and other ailments. P was the primary caregiver and visited him nearly every day, bringing him donuts and muffins and worrying about every aspect of his care. Was he eating enough? Were staff members making sure he was clean? And why did his pants keep disappearing in the laundry? P found much to complain about and worried that she was not doing enough, that she should never have put him in this facility and that her siblings were not participating in his care or even visiting him that often.

This father, an alcoholic for most of his life, had been verbally and emotionally abusive, especially to his sons and to his wife. Now, his dementia had turned him into a sweet, gentle man. P felt that for the first time she was having a real relationship with her father, something she had always longed for. He was very happy to see her, although sometimes he forgot who she was. It gave her genuine pleasure when he responded to the donuts she brought him or smiled at her when she visited.

Facing his imminent death, P began to think about the losses in her life. She missed her mother deeply and felt that she had not adequately mourned her death. She had recently lost her career due to an injury and perhaps had too much time in which to worry about her father; she was slow to accept that he was going to die because it frightened her. Even though she was a person of faith and had a religious frame in which to place concepts of eternal life, she worried that her father and mother would not be together.

Several months before her father died, her younger brother was diagnosed with an aggressive form of lung cancer. P descended into a dark place in which she constantly questioned why this was happening to her and to her family. It seemed so unfair and she was not sure how she could handle both deaths at the same time. She sprang into action, trying to get her brother treatment while monitoring her father's decline. She joined a class action suit so that the family could be compensated for her brother's cancer. And she expressed her fear that now her father, her mother and her brother might not be together. Why was God taking away all the people she loved? Why could she not prevent it?

Through journaling, P began to imagine her mother in heaven. She wrote details of how peaceful her mother was and began to imagine her father dying a peaceful death which would end his suffering. She wrote a story of her mother sending a beam of heavenly light down to meet her father and imagined him floating along this light to join his wife. As P read the story, I invited her to imagine herself surrounded by this light as well. Even though this story could not explain why this was happening to her family, the exercise in imagining her parents as peaceful and connected made the question of "Why?" less important.

Who am I?

Along with the emotional shattering of grief, the roles that you play in your life are irrevocably shifted. When your spouse dies, your identity as wife or husband, lover, friend and partner seems voided. When a parent dies, a part of who you are seems to die with them. If you have lost a child, your identity as a parent is adversely affected. This section contains strategies for discovering who you were, who you are now and who you want to be. In *addition, there is a focus on qualities, traits and abilities that are also part of one's identity in order to use these qualities as resources.*

๛

"Who am I?" the widow asked me. She was tall, with thick, wavy, grey hair. She wore a purple shirt with a gold linked chain; her glasses were rectangular with purple sides. "I left my parent's house when I was 20, and I've been the Doctor's Wife, ever since. We were married for 51 years. I don't know who I am." She turned her hands up in the air, shrugged her shoulders, then dabbed her left eye beneath the glass. "I didn't think I would cry," she said, surprised.

We were sitting in her comfortable living room, on opposite low green chairs. In addition to couches and lamps, the room had several tables filled with dozens of family photographs. Floor-to-ceiling shelves lined the walls, packed with books and a collection of Chinese jade and ceramics, partially hidden by more photographs. Several of them were family groupings of several generations. One showed a happy young bride dressed in a high-necked, long-sleeved gown, from which I surmised that the family was orthodox. I asked about her family and learned something about her life, including the children they had raised together and how many grandchildren she now had. I gently suggested that the woman married to the doctor, who parented the children and shared his life for so many years, was right here, sitting across from me. Even though she felt like she had lost her identity, she was still there.

The widow told me that she wandered through the house, not quite believing that her husband was truly gone.

According to her, she was in denial during the hospice process, convincing herself over and over that another treatment would work. Since her husband's retirement nine and a half years before, they had spent nearly every moment together. Then she said that when she starts to break down, she remembers something important. She remembers that she is still standing, here in her house, with comfort and good food to eat, with her children and grandchildren nearby. She is even having company for dinner. She is, in fact, alive.

I get it. Even though she is going through the motions, she feels as if everything in her life is off-kilter. Her identity is so connected to her definition as the Doctor's Wife that it is hard for her to think of herself as simply that, her own self. She has never thought this way, and coming to terms with the new reality of her life now will take time. And this is something that people often don't want to hear in the early part of bereavement.

This identity crisis of grief is quite prevalent and not only for widows. Parents who have lost a child, particularly an only child, wonder if it means they are no longer parents. A client of mine questioned whether he was still a father now that his daughter was gone. He also struggled with missing her as a sounding board to discuss his work, which she avidly supported. Now he felt a loss of purpose, which caused him to question his very reason for existing and continuing to create the work he used to love. He struggled to find a sense of himself in this new world without her and said that he did not feel whole in any aspect of his life. The great "Who am I?" question loomed large, but just like the doctor's wife, he was beginning to recognize that expressing his continued love for his daughter and finding ways to re-engage in work that she supported would eventually lead him back to a renewed sense of self.

A woman in one of our support groups described herself as having six siblings and then she corrected herself, saying, "No, there are only five now." We gently told her that she still had that sixth brother even though he was dead. He had not been erased and would always be a part of her family unit even though he was no longer here in the physical world.

When Alby died, I really struggled with the fact that I was no longer married. I struggled with the feeling that my personality was in shards on the ground and I really felt that I did not know who I was anymore. I drew a rudimentary touch drawing to represent myself, surrounded by swirls and spirals to represent the various threads of my identity. Then I wrote the different answers to the question of "Who am I?"

Wife? I took that one out and wept for a while.

How do we cope with this sense of lost identity? When we look at ourselves through external definitions, it is hard to define that illusive sense of Self. If we feel shattered by grief, it is hard to know where to begin, how to rediscover who we really are, apart from the roles of being someone's wife, sibling, parent or friend. Now that they have died, these bonds seem broken.

If you are feeling a loss of identity because of this death, can you investigate the ways that you define yourself? Can you notice how part of your identity is bound up in relation to other people and yet the larger part of who you are is wholly you, a sum of your relationships, experiences and your personality?

When Alby died, I felt myself broken into a million pieces. The metaphor of these shards as pieces of my personality was a useful one. It gave me the opportunity to examine who I was in the past and who I was in the moment of this explosion in my life. I thought about my life and my experiences as a child and teenager. I considered how I operated in relationships, to my siblings, my children and how I was in my marriage. I thought and I wrote about what I was good at and what ways of being and behaving that could perhaps be shaped differently. As I considered the events in our marriage as well as other times in my life, it occurred to me that the process of putting myself back together again could be healing and could even provoke some growth.

In between bouts of crying and feeling as if I could not get out of bed, I reviewed my life. I reviewed our marriage and I decided that, for the most part, it had been very positive. I felt that we had been successful together and that I had learned how to give and receive love unconditionally. His death had introduced a level of compassion for others that was deeper than I had felt before because I had never known such pain. I also considered parts of my character that could stand a little adjusting, such as my fiery nature and my tendency to be somewhat snappy at times.

What I am suggesting is that when life breaks you open, coming back to wholeness is a process by which you can grow. While the circumstances are probably not at all to your liking or what you wished for, there is still a great opportunity as you reflect on who you were, who you are and who you want to be. Later on, in Chapter 6, 'Exploring the Past to Experience the Future', there is another creative exercise which can help you identify aspects of yourself and learn how to weave yourself into a more beautiful, stronger and compassionate "tapestry" as you continue to live.

Right now, you might consider who you are by looking at your external definitions as well as identifying qualities, strengths and even weaknesses, as you perceive them.

"Who am I?" portrait

You will need: drawing paper, pastels, crayons or colored pencils.

For this exercise, it is important to remember that you are not drawing a self-portrait for anyone else but you. The purpose of this is self-discovery and healing, not to make a picture that can be hung on the wall or in a museum. Of course, if you like your finished drawing, feel free to hang it up!

Close your eyes for a few minutes and focus on your breathing. Put your hands to your face and trace your own features lightly with your fingers. Open your eyes and draw your face, without worrying about being accurate or realistic.

When you have finished your portrait, look at it for a while and ask yourself,

"Who am I?"

You probably will come up with many answers to this question. Write whatever words come to your mind on the portrait, inside it, around it, within the hair or wherever you wish. Use different colors if that feels right. Fill the drawing with as many words that answer this question as possible.

When you are done, study your self-identity portrait. Notice the words that make up who you are.

During my internship at Visiting Nurse Service of New York, I assisted in a workshop called "Writing and Bereavement" led by a retired *New York Times* reporter. We were instructed to draw a large circle on the page, then fill it with one run-on sentence about our loss. After we finished, some people shared what they had written and everyone in the room listened respectfully to each other. There was enough pain, subdued and channeled as it was through the writing, for me to wonder if my trembling was due to the chilly room or the grief all around me.

Another widow began to talk with me. She tearfully said repeatedly that she wanted to find a way to "move on." When she discovered that our stories were similar, both of us widowed in the middle of marriage with teenaged children, she quickly slid over next to me, putting her hand on my arm and asking me intensely, "How do I do this? I want this pain to stop. Do you have a boyfriend?" I acknowledged that I did.

The fact that I started dating someone changed nothing about my sadness and sense of dislocation. It was still the overriding "issue," filling my thoughts with "Why?" and "What?" and "How?" questions. Even as I attended museum openings, met new people, prepared to travel to far-off places, my life felt like an unknown territory. The recurring thought was "Whose life am I in?" Because even though I was actually doing new things, it did not feel congruent. Everything felt a bit off, as if I were in it and still observing it, checking every corner for clues on how to proceed. I was adrift in some dark water, knowing how to swim but unable to feel the bottom and searching with one foot for some stability. When I mentioned how groundless I felt, the new boyfriend said this:

"The groundlessness is the ground."

Not exactly what I wanted to hear. I was desperate for solidity; I was desperate for control. If death taught me anything, it was that I was not in control even when I believed I was. This realization, along with the wavering, groundless ground that I unsteadily tried to walk on, caused me to consider a fundamental truth in my own way of being: I often did try to control things, including events and even people. Was this a good trait or a bad trait? Was this a useless endeavor?

As I considered whether I could stand on groundless ground, I was reminded of a C.S. Lewis story. In the 1950s he wrote a science fiction trilogy, called the "Space Trilogy" or the "Cosmic Trilogy." The middle book, called *Perelandra*, takes place on the planet Venus, which is covered with water. The land floats and, because it is not rooted to the planet, standing on the floating islands is a difficult task until the characters get used to the rolling beneath their feet. Alternately, I thought of being on the ocean on a ship. At first it was hard to walk across the deck as the boat swayed up and down. Once I was on a ship near a hurricane and the boat heaved back and forth as well as vertically. I challenged myself to walk around on deck without falling. This required a softening in the knees, a widening of arms for balance and a different approach to walking. It was more like a subtle dance.

The groundless ground refers to the impermanence of life. It refers to the fact that just when we think we know what will happen next, we discover that we don't. This is startling and unsettling and if we become anxious about it, we try to resist. Resistance causes a stiffening of the body, a tightness in the chest and neck. Resistance causes us to wrap our arms around ourselves in protection. This very resistance, this rigid attempt to be strong and upright even though the ground is roiling, can very likely cause us to fall. You cannot regain your balance if you are inflexible.

I did not like hearing that the groundlessness is the ground but slowly, it dawned on me that this was true and also that this truth did not have to be frightening. So I did not know what would happen. I did not know what shape my life might take. If I softened my stance, I might become more open to the possibilities. If I relaxed and simply experienced the rolling of emotion, of change, of uncertainty, I might become more comfortable in my life now. I might let go of trying to control what cannot be controlled.

Bereavement has its own movement and as we travel on its unknown paths, we learn how to navigate. In the beginning, we have no idea how to deal with the sorrow, with the secondary losses of family position, roles we used to define ourselves by, of perhaps having to take on responsibilities we didn't have before. Grief comes with its own metaphors which can explain some of its experience.

The literal movement of grief can be explained like this: Grief moves like a rollercoaster as it plunges down into the depths and up again. Grief is a wave you don't see coming up behind you, crashing down on the ocean floor, tumbling you upon the rocks and shells on the bottom. Gasping for breath, you rise to the surface, only to have another wave overtake you. If you feel as if you are drowning in your grief, remember that you know how to swim. Relax as you get knocked down and you will find yourself floating to the surface. If it takes too much energy to swim back to the metaphorical shore, flip over on your back and float for a while. Take a few deep breaths to calm yourself.

One client described her grief as a whirlpool. She felt as if she were being pulled down into the center of it, in a teeming ocean of sorrow and anxiety. It was very frightening and she was afraid that she would not be able to recover. I asked her if she could imagine the color of the whirlpool and she said it was black.

Handing her a large piece of paper and a black pastel crayon I asked her to draw the whirlpool. She vehemently drew a large black spiral in the center of the page. As she sat back to look at it, I asked if she could imagine the shore. She chose a light brown pastel and drew a line for the shore. She placed a red circle within the whirlpool to represent herself. Then I asked if she could figure out how to get out. She thought she could swim in a straight line, but in talking about it, she realized that she would need to swim around in larger and larger concentric circles in order to reach the edge of the eddy. She drew this with the red pastel and then she said that she could imagine a life guard on the shore who was holding out a hook. She imagined herself grabbing it and pulling herself up on the sand.

She took a deep breath and surveyed her drawing. "I feel a lot better," she commented. She had used a visual representation of her emotions and had called on her own imagination to help her discover that she had the capability to survive the feeling that she was being sucked down by grief.

Working with metaphors

What is a metaphor for your grief? Is it a whirlpool, a wave, a volcano? Create a visual of this metaphor by imagining what it looks and feels like, using colored pencils or pastels. After gathering materials and paper, close your eyes, imagine your metaphor of grief. Without thinking too much, scribble or draw it out on the page. Imagine where you are inside the metaphor and if you are stuck somewhere, imagine and draw yourself out. You can add any tool or assistant to help you in the picture you make.

When you are done, respond to the metaphor of your grief, noticing how you feel now that you have imagined your way back to safety.

The death of someone you care about is a holistic experience in that it affects you emotionally, psychologically, spiritually and physically. As your emotions course through your body, all kinds of adverse reactions can be stimulated. Some people have terrible stomach aches or headaches. Some feel tightness in the chest or even pains in the area of their heart as if their heart was literally breaking. Some are hungry all the time; some cannot remember to eat. Some people want to sleep for hours on end; some of us (like me) have trouble sleeping for more than two hours at a time. These reactions are the body's way of releasing the shock, but they can be alarming. If we can recognize these physical reactions as part of our body's way of coping, we can find ways to mitigate their effects. While sitting on the edge of the abyss, notice what is happening inside your physical and emotional field.

As the initial shock of the death begins to subside, and as we continue to process the "What?" and "Why?" and "Who?" of it, we also focus on the "How?" How will we ever be able to survive this pain? Where is help to be found?

CHAPTER 3

H

HELP! How Can I Get Through This?

Along with accepting the reality of the loss, grievers need concrete strategies to process grief, including inspiration from other people's experiences. This chapter offers practical and creative ideas on how to manage aspects of mourning.

> *This was not the plan.*
> *This was not*
> *supposed*
> *to*
> *happen.*

How is this possible
that you
are now
not here?

~ (PERSONAL JOURNAL, MAY 2005)

No one knows how to grieve. Even though everyone dies, we have no instruction manual that tells us how to get through the pain, how to take care of all the practical things that need attention while we can't even think straight for more than two minutes, if that. And we wish we had instructions. We wish there was some kind of road map to help us navigate the alien landscape that is our world now. We need help.

If grief has any rules at all, it is this: Always carry a box of tissues with you. You're going to need them.

I was alone when he died and in a strange place. I couldn't think straight, in fact, I couldn't breathe correctly and had to be given oxygen. We had planned to visit with an old teacher of ours later that week so she was the first person I called. I don't remember what I said; maybe I just repeated, "He's dead." She said she would call me right back and when she did, she asked, "Is there anyone who can be with you now?" She planned to come to see me the next day.

Our friend Missy's decision to ask someone to drive her to Santa Fe to be with me is an example of someone helping without my asking. I had no idea what I needed anyway so am eternally grateful for actions like this. Help appeared in odd places and in some cases was arranged by my sisters and my close friends. For instance, every night for two weeks, someone drove up to our house at 5 o'clock, carrying food for dinner. This was a great alternative to an influx of random frozen casseroles that we would have had to figure out. There were many people who helped without asking questions, including the father of a friend of my youngest. He noticed that my mailbox stand was broken and asked if it would be alright to replace it. And when I said yes with thanks, he was there within an hour because he had already built us a new one.

Not everyone is so lucky to have a community rally around or to have the benefit of a lot of siblings who just show up or call every night. And sometimes, the people that you thought would be there to help don't come around. This is very strange and jarring but it is a fact. Death is scary and people can react oddly to it. I had a friend who did not call me for several months and when she finally did, she apologized. She acknowledged that the death of Alby at age 50 was so frightening for her because he was the same age as her husband. She, 15 years older than him, was caught up in worry about mortality, either hers or his. She said she was not proud of it, but she simply could not call.

People generally react to others out of their own life experiences and sometimes this causes them to respond with compassion and kindness but unfortunately, sometimes not. This can add a layer of anger and frustration to your own grief when you have expectations. It can be helpful to remember that many simply do not know what to do or say. They might be upset by the death as well and are having trouble imagining how they would handle it. Perhaps they try to think of something that might fix or take away your pain, which is, of course, impossible. And sometimes what people say, springing from a desire to help, is actually hurtful.

When this comes from a person you expected would be more sensitive, such as a sibling or long-term friend, it adds another challenge.

It is a good practice to understand this is where most "off" comments come from. You may encounter an urge to push people away, but consider this: They just don't know what to say or do. If you are able to, accept help and support from those that step up, and let go of expectations that don't come to fruition. As a colleague from a hospice used to say, "Bless them and release them." If possible, send a little compassion their way because there is no way they just can get it. And I wouldn't want to wish this experience on them so that they do.

How to grieve

I can't tell you how to do this. I can't tell you how you will feel in the morning when you wake up after sleeping a bit. It is very likely that you will open your eyes and suddenly realize, all over again, that he is dead. You might feel the crushing weight of this sudden blast of reality, pushing you back on the mattress, filling your eyes with tears and your throat with a suppressed scream.

Every morning for nearly six months, I woke up to the sound of birds. My first thought as I surfed the narrow distance between dreaming and waking was, "How peaceful." Second thought—slam. A sudden icy cold would emanate from my core, my arms spread out on the pillow would wrap around me, my hands to my face. Flooded with sorrow, my eyes would fill and my throat constrict.

The third thought was of disturbed wonder. How could the birds continue to sing when he was not here to listen? How did the sun rise, day after day, taking us further away from his life? How would I be able to figure out my own life now, without him, with these teenagers to guide? *How will I get out of this bed?*

There were no answers to these questions. There was only the fact of the birds, the dawn and the tasks of the morning. My teenagers needed to get up and go to school or at least give it a try. There were exams for them to complete. My son had been selected to attend Boys State, a weekend civics lesson and he wanted to go. He didn't want to go but then again, he really did. My oldest daughter had started her summer job at the pharmacy and she needed to get up and go to work. The little one would go to school and several times a week, call me by 11 am and say, "I can't do this."

How do we do this? This question looms large when heavy emotions are interfering with any attempt at normal functioning. Until you are inside of it, there are no guides that can truly help you navigate this alien landscape that is now your life. How do you get through this pain, how do you find some sense of who you are, now that your world has been broken apart?

Getting through the first few months of grief

While the first two weeks after Alby died are etched into my mind and probably into my cellular structure, I can barely remember how I got through the first few months. Shock was something of a blessing, allowing me to float from day to day, struggling to take care of what needed to be done. There was a lot to do as it was the beginning of my catering season and my first event was just 18 days after he died.

I was barely functioning, on auto-pilot alternating with extreme bouts of sobbing. I could barely think, so I decided not to try to think too much. I reminded myself several times a day to take things moment by moment. If the next moment found me staring off into space, I would wait for the next one and try to make it more productive. I relied on my staff, friends and family to be with me, keep me as much on track as I could manage and to pick up some of the slack when it was clear that I was literally out of my mind with grief.

Try to pay attention to what is most needed, what your body is calling for while your heart is breaking. Let go of the expectation that you will function normally; you won't be able to for a long time. Allow this, adjust for it, take steps to minimize stress and make space for your feelings to sort themselves out; and when you can, give them full expression.

Helping yourself through

Here are some ideas for helping yourself get through the early days:

1. *Take care of yourself. Remember to eat. If you are having trouble with this, ask someone close to you to remind you or to bring you something simple and tasty.*

Drink soothing teas, such as peppermint, chamomile, licorice or just something you really like. Drink lots of water to replace the liquid lost in your tears.

2   Be gentle with yourself. Right now, it really is all about you, what you need and how you feel. If you are tired, sleep. Let yourself cry; it is better to release feelings than bottle them up.

3.   When people ask if there is anything they can do, give them a task. Have them bring you food, pick up the newspaper. Ask them to come over and sit with you if you like them, or send them to do something you don't want to take care of.

4.   Pay no attention to anyone who tells you what you "should" do or what you "should" be feeling. They do not know.

5.   Make a list of things that must be done, in order of importance. If you do one of these items a day, you will have accomplished something good.

6.   Just as you must allow yourself to feel awful and express these feelings, it is equally important to allow for some normalcy. Taking a walk outside even if it is only for a short time can be relaxing as can listening to music, sitting with friends and family and sharing funny stories about your loved one.

Sitting with your grief/ walking away for a while

We cannot wallow in sorrow all the time. The dual process model describes the oscillation between loss orientation (feeling sad, longing, depression and intrusive thoughts) and restorative orientation (activities of daily living, life changes, doing new things). It is important to feel grief but it is equally important to set it aside for a while in order to heal.

Research into how we grieve has come up with many models to help us. The tug and pull between being focused on coping with the effects of loss and coping with paying the bills, going to work, taking care of your family and yourself is called the "Dual Process Model of Coping with Bereavement," developed by psychologists Margaret Stroebe and Hans Schut (1999). It demonstrates how we oscillate back and forth between doing and feeling, between action and being. Some people tend to be more active in their approach to grief, plunging back into daily activities and finding that keeping busy seems to keep the sorrow at bay. This side of the Dual Process is called the "Restoration Orientation." Others spend more time in the emotional realm, which is referred to as the "Loss Orientation." But every bereaved person fluctuates between these two aspects. This Dual Process explains that feeling of being split between trying to "get on with your life" and wading in the quagmire of your sorrow. Neither orientation feels normal, especially when your life is cracked and broken. How can you accomplish these seemingly opposite realities? How can you allow your feelings their expression and still take care of things that are important to accomplish?

There is a natural tendency to oscillate between wallowing in states of feeling and taking care of the ordinary business of life. Many people must return to work shortly after the death of a loved one, and find themselves in a weird situation where they are expected to perform normally, as if nothing happened. This often feels misaligned with what is authentic for the griever. Add to this the "kind" comments of co-workers and acquaintances who applaud the brave front as a demonstration of "strength." On the other hand, re-engaging in the tasks of daily living, including immersing yourself in your work, has benefits in that it gives you something else to do and something else to think about. Yet, the death and the hole in your life is always present, even as you go through the motions of doing your work, doing your life, taking care of business as best you can.

Not everyone feels that the death of someone is an extremely adverse experience. We may not have had a good relationship with this person or there might be mitigating circumstances. Death affects each person differently and the areas affected vary. If the death was long expected, the level of upheaval in our own lives could be minimal or we may be surprised to find that knowing death was imminent did not make coping afterwards any easier. It is more important to recognize that your reactions to your own grief are influenced by many factors and will also impact many areas of your life. Allowing yourself to feel grief deeply and also to walk away from it for a while will help you cope. In an informal survey of bereaved people, I asked if people felt shattered by death and in what areas of their lives felt the most broken. Respondents were allowed to check all that applied. I found that 75 percent said they felt shattered by the death and nearly 69 percent felt personally shattered. Of the nearly 80 people who responded, almost half agreed that it took longer than they expected, nearly a year, for this feeling to pass.

An unreal reality

How do we move through our daily routines in a world that feels unreal? For months I floated mindlessly through the day, forgetting what I was doing, unable to complete tasks or think logically. Yet there was work to be done, teenagers to encourage and support, a college kid who needed permission to re-engage in her school life. My work was intermittent but intense and I usually kept much of the tasks in my head. No longer. My lists grew and were filled with minutiae to make sure that I did not forget to transfer the credit cards, pay the mortgage, figure out the health insurance, meet with a potential client, pick up a kid, buy groceries.

Many people feel as if the world has taken on an odd, muted shade, its edges dulled and somewhat amorphous. Your brain is in a fog and everything around you feels murky too. Coupled with wildly fluctuating emotions, you might feel as if you have lost control of your life. One way to help you through this syndrome is to take control of small parts of your daily life.

What needs to be accomplished during the day? How much of this is really important, sort of important, neutral or not important at all? Do you need to call people to let them know about the death? Do you need to take any action with institutions such as banks, doctors or other community resources? If you are going back to work, do you need to get a haircut, take clothes to the dry cleaners or polish your shoes?

These small daily tasks can seem daunting when you are inside the fog of grief. Make a list of things that need to be done so you will remember. Add to your list as you remember other items. Take a look at what is absolutely necessary and what can be put off. Number or color code them so that you are aware of priorities and then check off items as they are completed. If you manage to check off one item a day, consider it worthwhile. List-making is a good way to keep yourself on track when you can't think.

Sometimes the person who died managed many practical things that we haven't done in a while, even though we are perfectly capable of doing so. This is often the case when one is widowed after a long marriage; we tend to divide tasks. Couples often split chores, with one person handling finances and another taking care of certain household chores such as mowing the lawn or shopping and cooking. I have had elderly male clients whose wives took care of the checkbook and all the investing and they don't even know where the bank is. I have had young widowed clients who were used to taking care of the children and all their appointments but dissolved in tears because the broken toilet was too much for them to handle.

I have visited newly bereaved people in their homes and found their dining room tables covered with piles of paper as they tried to figure out what bills to pay and when, what oil company to call to fill the tank for the winter, which bank account to close. If you are overwhelmed dealing with paperwork that perhaps was handled by the person who died, enlist a friend or a professional to help you get organized. Speak to the bank manager and ask for their assistance. Don't be embarrassed by asking questions of professionals. Make an appointment with your doctor for a check-up and while you are there, ask any questions you might have.

I don't want to admit it: that my life as I knew it is over and
that I am totally alone with no prospects of not being so. I know
this does not mean that I have no future but I can't see it.
In my new Be Here Now state of mind,
where I sit
is
nowhere.

~ (PERSONAL JOURNAL, AUGUST 2005)

In a well-appointed living room, surrounded by family photos and colorful paintings, a widow sat, a slice of pizza on a plate in her lap. Carved cabinets from their travels to China flanked the walls along with upholstered love seats covered with large pillows that had to be moved out of the way in order to sit. This woman had been married for nearly 50 years to a successful businessman who wrote poetry and painted in his spare time. She herself had two Master's degrees and a habit of talking only about herself and how his death had shattered her life. Despite a career in education, she presented as a fragile person in need of a lot of attention. During her husband's illness, she loudly proclaimed that she would not be able to live without him. When his poetry was mentioned, she talked about stories she had written. Her lifelong habit of making everything about herself was frustrating to her children, who had little patience with her grieving process, especially since it interfered with their own. As the hospice grief counselor, I was there to help them all but mostly, I was there for her. One of her daughters was in the room, trying to think of ways for her mother to exercise some independence, thinking that this would get her out of her "funk." She sat next to her, making suggestions for how her mother could cope. "You really should join a gym, Mom," she insisted. If she only went to the gym, she would not be so sad and she would get out and meet new people. Her mother looked at her in surprise, then back at me. She had not yet begun to drive herself places and the idea of joining a gym seemed like being asked to jump onto the nearest spaceship and go to Mars. Ignoring her daughter, in a small, shaking voice, she asked, "How do I do this?"

I looked at the slice of pizza and back at her. Softly, I answered, "You can approach your grief like you approach that slice of pizza. You won't pick up that whole piece and shove it into your mouth, will you? How will you eat it?"

She looked down at the slice of pizza and considered this for a moment. "I guess I will just have to eat it one bite at a time."

We often think too far ahead. When you are grieving, you cannot imagine what your future will be like, now that your loved one is no longer in it. When the relationship has existed for much of your lifetime, it is even harder to envision. Trying to predict the future, or even trying to imagine it, creates panic and even fear. There is a worry that if you get up and go into your own life, you will be leaving your loved one behind. Will you forget about them as you become involved in something new? Will they become less important? If you laugh again or have happy experiences, does this mean that you no longer care about them?

These kinds of thoughts are very common in the early months of bereavement. As we sit inside our cocoon of emotional reaction to the death, the outside world and its possibilities seem blank, even frightening. Before they died, we made plans. Now, making plans seems almost like a betrayal. But if you think about the plans you made in the past, did they always turn out the way you planned them? Perhaps you were planning to go to the movies and on the way, you had a flat tire. The process of changing this tire took up so much time that once your car was ready to drive again, you had missed the beginning of the movie. You changed your plan. Perhaps you decided to go out to dinner instead or to just go back home. Either way, the plan you made and what really happened were two different things. We plan and then things change.

Now, when you cannot see ahead too far, how would it be if you just thought about this moment? How would it be if, when thinking about the future, you only thought about the next hour? Or perhaps, just this one day? If you are having trouble getting out of bed, lie back and consider these two choices: One, you might be able to stay in bed. What would happen if you did? Would the world end because you decided not to get up today? Perhaps there is something important you must do today—perhaps you have an appointment to meet a friend or you are supposed to go to the doctor's. Maybe you have to go to work or you might lose your job. You then consider choice number Two, which is making yourself get out of the bed, even though you don't feel like it. How do you do this? No one awakens, then jumps up after a night of sleep, fully clothed, teeth brushed, hair combed, keys in hand. How do you get out of bed? You stretch, pull the covers off and turn so your feet go down to the floor. Place your feet on the ground and stand up. There. You got up. Good for you.

We don't think about the steps it takes to get up in the morning but when you are feeling as if you can't, noticing every movement, every gesture, is a way to accomplish it. I recommend congratulating yourself on a job well done at each step of the way, because this small thing, something that you have been doing since your parents stopped picking you up and carrying you everywhere, seems so difficult at this time in your life. When you feel as if you cannot get out of bed and then you do, you have climbed over a hurdle. And now that you are awake and standing, you can continue on to the next step, perhaps having a cup of tea or coffee, taking a shower, getting dressed and getting ready to start your day. If at any point in this arduous process of confronting your day you begin to feel overwhelmed, sit down. Notice how you are feeling. Take a deep breath and when you are ready, continue.

There will probably be a voice in your head berating yourself, saying, really? You used to be so competent; you awoke and got up without much thought before. Why can't you do that now? What is wrong with you, anyway?

Is that voice a helpful one or not? Grief is hard enough to get through without telling yourself you are not doing it right. The most important thing to remember when you consider how to grieve is that since each person is unique, each person's process is unique as well. The way you get through will be different than mine or your neighbor's. The most important way to get through this difficult time is to listen to yourself. Notice how you feel and respond to it. Notice if there is a constriction in your chest or throat when you start to do something. This is a clear message from your body and your heart that the task you are about to take on might not be the right one. And if you notice an uncomfortable reaction to the task at hand and it absolutely must be completed, take some time to get there. Go slowly through each step leading up to what needs to be done. See if there might be some choices you can make that help you. Ask for help from someone you trust, if you can.

It is important to acknowledge to yourself that you have the right to mourn. You have the right to express how you feel and no one can compel you to be "strong" or stoic. People may admire this quality and hope that you will stay calm, carry on and actually not bother them with random weeping or long stories about your loved one and their death, how you have been affected by it, and so on. It is, of course, a question of choice; there are indeed times where it is not appropriate to talk about this and there are indeed people with whom sharing is not particularly emotionally safe for you. Still, you deserve to experience this event and its impact on you and your life.

How you get through your grief will be different than how I got through mine. But I do have some ideas to share which you might find helpful.

First, pay attention to what is happening within you. Are you having trouble concentrating? Are you distracted? Bringing yourself to the present moment can help redirect your scattered brain. Do this by taking a few moments to regroup and asking yourself these two questions:

Where am I?

What time is it?

If you answered the first question with "I am at work," this is not the right answer for this question. Of course, this may actually be where you are but the real answer is this:

"I am HERE."

By naming where you are as HERE, you begin to notice this one moment. Name where HERE is to you: "I am sitting at my desk; I am wearing a blue suit; one foot is on the ground and the other is tucked underneath me with its shoe off. My hands are folded in my lap. I am HERE." Notice your body and how it feels. Take a deep breath and repeat to yourself,

"I am HERE." Breathe again. Notice a little more about the here and now of where you are.

Ask yourself the second question: "What time is it?" Don't look at your watch or the clock on the wall or think about a deadline you might have looming above you. What time is it?

The time is NOW. This moment, no other. In this moment, notice where you are and repeat the answers to these two questions.

"I am HERE. The time is NOW." Take a few moments and breathe in the here and nowness of this moment. This should help you feel more grounded and focused.

I had work too. When he died, I was a caterer and that summer was the most successful one I had ever had in terms of bookings, with 11 weddings between May and October. The first wedding was two hours away, 18 days after he died. One hundred and thirty people were attending, with a Filipino bride and a red-headed doctor groom who insisted on building a pirate ship out of cake mix with pretzel masts and containers of store-bought icing. The wedding cake I had made for them was carrot with white chocolate mousseline, topped with a single, giant pink peony. It rained on this wedding, which fit the mood I was in, which I only let out in the corners of the kitchen tent. My staff did everything and I pretended to be in charge. All three of the kids were working this event because I needed them there with me.

It was easy to put on my caterer/wedding planner smile and move smoothly through the crowd, appearing to direct things. It was easy because no one focuses on the caterer; everyone is looking at the bride. Everyone is drinking, dancing, and eating the food (which was still delicious in spite of my collapsing several times during the cooking process). I complimented the dress; I served the Israeli salad that honored the groom's Jewish roots; I dramatically blew at the clouds in an attempt to make the rain go away. Inside that kitchen tent though, I was on the ground in tears.

If you have to go back to work, you may find that there will be several times during the day where you simply cannot. You simply cannot do whatever it is you are supposed to be doing. To cope with waves of emotion when they wash over you at "inappropriate" times, develop a list of options.

Do you have some colleagues you can trust in your workplace? Let them know that you are grieving and that sometimes you might need to take a moment or two to regroup.

Investigate a couple of safe places to retreat to. If you are lucky to have a private office with its own door, you can simply close it for a few minutes. Inside, you can use grounding techniques to calm yourself. You can also allow yourself time to have a short cry to release pent-up emotions.

If you don't have an office of your own at work, the bathroom might be a good alternative. Walk, don't run. Practice quiet, deep inhales and exhales as you walk there. Go inside, find a private space and take a break.

Go outside for a few minutes. Breathe in the air. Breathe out your pain.

Call a friend or a family member who is sympathetic and will listen. Don't call someone who will tell you to be strong or to get on with it, whatever "it" is. Call someone who will understand that you need to vent for a minute, will listen to you say, "I miss her sooooooo much right now." You might consider telling a few people in advance that you will do this and advise them to listen and to simply say, "I know" instead of going into a narrative about how they felt when their dog died. Not to disparage anyone who grieves when a beloved pet dies but it is not on a par with a husband, parent, sibling, child or any *human* loss.

Being grateful

Even though you are in so much pain you can barely breathe, finding small things to be grateful for helps you get through the day. Focusing on what you have accomplished during the day, even if it is simply getting out of your room and eating a couple of meals, helps you encourage your way through the grief process. The technique of making a "Grateful List" is calming and reminds you that there are still good things in your world. You can try this in the morning when you are having difficulty getting out of bed. You might be grateful that you slept for at least part of the night. You could be grateful for the outdoor sounds you hear. Perhaps you might be grateful for the friend you will talk with later or even have a cup of tea with. Name a few things you are grateful for when you wake up in the morning.

Making a Grateful List before you go to sleep is also a good technique and will help you relax, calm your spinning mind and soften your emotions. Be grateful for the day and name several small things that happened during the day. Try the Grateful List technique at whatever time of day seems right for you. If you wish, you can write your list in a journal or on a pad kept near you, on your nightstand.

Gratitude

What are you grateful for? Commit to answering this question every day for a week. Make a list, and beginning with "I am grateful for_____," list at least five things. They don't have to be huge things. Here is an example:

I am grateful for the sunshine.

I am grateful for my family.

I am grateful that I am still alive.

I am grateful for music.

I am grateful for the squirrel running up the tree, preparing for winter.

The importance of journaling

Another effective way to help you get through grief is to journal. I have always written in journals. I have filled notebooks with my worries and with burgeoning philosophy as I sought to discover the meaning of life as a teenager. I have splashed emotion on the pages of spiral-bound books, marbled composition books, steno pads, sketch books and any kind of paper I could grab. Creatively processing my thoughts through writing helps me clarify these musings and also helps calm my feelings.

Everyone has an inner world. Our interior "place" is in our mind, our heart and even in our body. We think our way through interpersonal relations and we feel our way through the morass of connection/disconnection and understanding and missing the point. Even in solitude, we think our way through each moment (well, at least I do!).

As a child, my inner world was rich with expression. My emotions were very strong and filled my small body with energy, which in turn needed channeling and focus. I released this energy through dance, music and writing. I never thought of myself as a writer although I have written nearly all my life. I am a person who is always making things—phrases of movement, a crocheted blanket or hat, a picture made of fabric and embroidery. Poems, distillations of events or encounters with fascinating people, written all in lower case à la ee cummings, filled the pages of my journals. My secret, inner world, my conflicts with certain family members, some unfortunate love affairs, a failed marriage, then a rich, wonderful marriage fill my pile of books. Some have plans for vacations and then observations made on those travels. Some are filled with stick figures and personal choreographic codes that became dances performed in small black box theaters or larger halls. Whole phrases of language or whole phrases of movement appeared in my brain and needed a place to reside—my journals were their home. I wrote my way through my emancipation from my family of origin and I wrote my way out of a crazy early marriage in which every possible relationship mistake was made. I grew through this writing and wrote advice to myself on how to change, how to commit, how to *be*. I filled pages with dreams, drawings and pictures to craft my future. I weighed pros and cons in relationships and decided how to parent. Some pages are of menu plans and recipes; some pages have phrases in different languages to connect to others when traveling.

It's funny that I never thought of myself as a writer. I have struggled with personal definitions whenever I shifted my focus, changing from describing myself as a musician who danced on the side to a DANCER in capital letters. I defined myself as a wife and mother and then I defined myself as a caterer. When I stopped dancing, I had difficulty with the loss of this definition, and a wise woman asked me a simple question. She asked, "Why do you need to define yourself by what you do? Can't you define yourself as Claudia?"

She was, of course, correct. Inside my journals, I define my life. Within the pages of my books, I explore who I am, how I feel and I discover How To Be.

Journaling is a proven way to help you process events and cope with all the emotions and thoughts spinning around in your head and in your body. When you write down your feelings and your ruminations in a book, it releases some of them from the inside to the outside. Once they are placed in the book, you can then close the cover and put it on a table or a shelf, metaphorically taking a break from all these thoughts and feelings. They are now contained inside the journal. Later, if you wish, you might visit your journal and the landscape of your grief; how you felt and reacted will be revealed anew. You might be able to see a progression; you may be able to notice how you have grown through the process of grieving this loss or change in your life.

Research has shown that writing in times of difficulty can be very beneficial. James Pennebaker (1997) conducted studies with university students where they were asked to write for 15 minutes every day for four days. Some of the students were asked to simply write about whatever they liked and some were directed to write specifically about a difficult or traumatic event in their lives. Another group was directed to vent emotions about a difficult event and another group was asked to write both facts and feelings. The researchers then followed these students and tracked the rate of illness over a period of time after the writing experiment. Through this tracking, Pennebaker proved that writing provided benefits to those who wrote about these troubling times in their lives. This group reported that they felt better about those traumas, that the act of writing about their difficult situations helped them feel a bit more resolved and less activated when they thought about those events. In fact, those who used their writing to vent emotions had a 50 percent lower rate of illness after the experiment. For the control group, writing offered little opportunity for change. This research, done in the 1980s, has generated what is now called the "Pennebaker Paradigm."

Writing in and of itself will not cure grief. In his book *Opening Up: The Healing Power of Expressing Emotion,* Pennebaker points out:

Exploring your deepest thoughts and feelings is not a panacea. If you are coping with death, divorce or other tragedy, you will not feel instantly better after writing. You should, however, have a better understanding of your feelings and emotions, as well as the objective situation you are in. In other words, writing should give you a little distance and perspective on your life. (Pennebaker, 1997, p.42)

Researchers continue to investigate how and why journaling helps. Pennebaker followed his studies and codified the benefits of journal writing in a new book along with John F. Evans, in which he identified specific areas that are affectively positively after writing about your distressing feelings. In addition to relieving stress, he found psychological and behavioral effects, both in mood changes and in the ability to function more effectively after writing.

Pennebaker says:

> Writing may make you sad for brief time after writing, but the long-term effects are far more positive. Across multiple studies, people who engage in expressive writing report feeling happier and less negative than they felt before writing. Similarly, reports of depressive symptoms, rumination and general anxiety tend to drop... (Pennebaker and Evans, 2014, p.11)

Wendy Lichtenthal (2017) and her research team at Sloan Kettering Memorial Hospital adapted Pennebaker's paradigm for bereavement, adding a prompt to include searching for meaning, or "benefit finding." This concept is a positive way of working through grief, developed by Dr. Robert Neimeyer of the University of Memphis. Dr. Neimeyer is a brilliant and compassionate therapist, professor and researcher, who believes that we must find ways to reconstruct our lives after the death of someone close to us. His explorations in how we find meaning after death have refocused thanatology and generated a field of evidence-based research on how we grieve and how we learn to live again after loss. Neimeyer's work relies greatly on narrative work, because he believes that meaning can be found in the story of the death and in the story of the relationship. He says:

> In the natural accommodation of loss, mourners commonly tack back and forth between these two stories, sharing them with receptive others in an effort to weave the death narrative into the larger story of their lives as a sad, but necessary transition, while drawing on and funding sustenance in the back story of their loved one's life, which continues to provide an attachment security as they reconstruct, rather than relinquish, their continuing bond. (Neimeyer, 2012b, p.86)

In other words, our stories become the basis for working through our feelings and discovering how to remain connected to the person who has died (continuing bonds) while figuring out how to reshape our lives after this death and find a sense of purpose again (meaning). Journaling can help us with this process and offers a safe container to hold these narratives.

When I first heard of this concept of making meaning after loss, I became quite angry. The idea that there could be a meaning in the death of my husband was initially abhorrent. How could his death be meaningful? He was not supposed to die four days after his 50th birthday! He was not supposed to suddenly leave us to carry on without him; I certainly was not supposed to be a single parent in the middle of raising our children. If making meaning was an act of making sense of his death, I was having none of it. I could not find meaning in the fact that he turned blue and was gone in an instant in that bed and breakfast in New Mexico.

Slowly, I began to look at this idea differently. As I entered a Master's program and then a grief counseling certification program, I began to see how *I* was making meaning in my life after he died. My desire to help others, awakened by my own experience, was an act of making meaning. My explorations of how to use creative ideas to help express what was happening led me to find meaning within those very expressions. Drawing circles, swirls and smudges in color to represent the emotions churning inside my body helped me give them voice. Reflecting on our marriage with its many benefits and its several hard times gave me a sense of satisfaction even as I mourned the loss of the relationship along with the loss of Alby. Learning to love some of the activities that he loved, such as gardening or simply being outside in nature, helped me continue to connect to him and there was a lot of meaning in that. So while I could not make sense of his actual death or why it happened, I could consider the gifts we shared and the gifts I received from being in that relationship and pay them forward. My own life could be rich with meaning both in spite of his death and in some ways because of it. I could not see this for a few years but I began to understand it as I became more comfortable with living with my grief. I began to find benefits within the pain and sorrow and I began to rekindle joy and learning in order to find meaning and a reason for *being*. And my journals provided me with containers in which to figure this all out.

A journal is not a diary. You don't have to begin each page with "Dear Diary, today I had oatmeal for breakfast"; unless, of course, you feel that reporting on your daily sustenance would be helpful to you. You don't have to write grammatically and you don't have to write in a straight line across the page. In fact, you don't even have to write! You can draw in your journal, collage inside it, paste photos of you and your dear departed one. You can explore what your life might look like in the pages of the journal by gathering pictures of something you'd like to do or learn or places you might like to visit. The journal is a vehicle to help you navigate your grief; and since it is your personal, private space, you can write or draw or scribble—there are no rules. You don't have to show it to anyone. If you write at 4 am, as I did when I was having trouble sleeping, you may not even be able to read it later. And, it is possible that as you move through this time in your life, your journal or journals will demonstrate to you later on that you have actually moved, shifted and digested some of the pain and sorrow.

I wrote in 12 journals that first year. Within them I processed the recurring dream in which I would be able to prove to the world that his death was a hoax. Within them I expressed my sadness and my anger. Inside my journals are poetic snippets, photos, poetry that we loved together or that moved me after he died. I never left home without a book in my purse, and my bed had a pile of them on his side. I used colored pens to portray different emotions.

A friend commented that I was externalizing my grief. At first I did not like this comment because I was exploring my inner world. But as I thought about it, I realized he was correct. I placed my reflections on my inner world within the pages of the journal which took some of the edge off the pain. Slowly, over several years, I began to find purpose in my life and while I could not find any meaning or benefit in the fact that he died, I could develop meaning in how I live after he died. There were so many benefits from being in a relationship with him and I wrote about these in the pages of my books.

First, find a nice book to write in. It could just be a yellow pad of paper or a simple composition book like school children use. Or you can go to a nice book or art store and find a blank book with a lovely cover, one that sort of speaks to you.

Choose something to write with that feels good in your hand. Try different kinds of pens to see what is most satisfying. This may sound like a lot to do but I have found that if the ink does not flow on the page and if the pen feels sticky, I do not enjoy writing. I also encourage you to get a set of colored pens so that you can match a color to an emotion.

Some people prefer to write on the computer, but I urge you to try writing in a book. The experience is different and you can be freer to add pictures, little line drawings or doodles, quotes, magazine cuttings—all the kinds of items that you would not be able to use if you are writing on a keyboard.

I highly recommend writing as an answer to "How do I get through this?" But I also recognize that this is easier for some, and many people don't know where to begin. In addition, many people get stuck in the thought that they don't know how to write. Try to let go of self-judging thoughts, if you can, and give yourself permission to feel what you feel and to give these feelings voice.

The inner critic

We all have one: an inner voice that critiques and criticizes, especially when we try someone new. Mine comes up sometimes when I am writing, telling me that I am being trite or ungrammatical. My inner critic gets very loud when I try to do something out of my comfort zone, such as drawing or virtually any kind of visual art on paper. My inner critic is quite powerful and has had the ability to stop me from engaging in expression that will actually feed my soul and might even be fun, artistic and meaningful. I have been guilty of allowing this inner voice to control some of my own process, which has interfered with completion of projects and caused a lot of useless self-doubt.

In my Master's program, we engaged in a wonderful exercise with the inner critic. We were asked to imagine this voice as an entity, to draw it and ask it its name. We were invited to enter into a dialog with this entity or person and ask it what it needed, what its real message was. Initially I was afraid to engage, because of course my inner critic was very busy telling me that I could not possibly draw its picture since I did not know how to draw anything and everything I drew was stupid, ugly, silly, etc., etc., etc.!

Bravely, I put pastels to paper, entered my imagination and drew this picture:

Whew! I was repulsed by her mean expression, her talon-like fingers waiting to tear me to shreds. I took a deep breath and asked her what her name was. In an ugly, rasping voice, she answered, "My name is Old Bat." Hmmm, I thought. That's not such a scary name; in fact, it's kind of funny! Really? That's the best you could come up with? I peered into my picture again. "So, Old Bat, what do you need?"

I closed my eyes and Old Bat melted. She melted into a little girl, sitting sadly on the floor. Someone had told her that she could not draw and she wanted to, so badly. She just wanted to color. My resistance to my inner critic also melted as I realized that she was really a wounded piece of my own inner child. "Here," I said to that part of me. "Here is a box of crayons. Why don't you sit over there and color for a while."

When you encounter inner resistance to any of the creative suggestions contained in this book, make a choice. You can of course decide not to try the suggestion. Or you can soften your resistance and explore the possibilities. If your inner critic is as loud as mine, you might try drawing its picture and having a little chat with it before you start.

The other problem with writing is that it is hard to get started. If you are not in the habit of scribbling down your thoughts on a page, it is difficult to figure out where to begin. So, I am offering you some prompts to get you started. There are many others but these ought to get you started. They are in no particular order and you might want to try only one or two of them. Just take a deep breath and give it a try. Writing can really help.

Easy writing ideas

1. The simplest way to start is to write how you are feeling, right now. Begin with "Today, I feel..." and go on from there. Don't be concerned about spelling or grammar.

2. Match a color to the feeling and write in that color.

3. Describe your day. Include how you felt and how you managed those feelings.

4. Write a letter to the person who died. Tell them about your day, how you feel about them being gone and how you are coping. This technique also helps when you wish you could tell them something important that has happened or if there is something you wish you had been able to tell them. Don't censor yourself – this is your private journal and you can be as honest as you need to be.

5. Answer this question: What do you miss the most? Reflect on it and write your answers in the journals. Then answer this question: What do you not miss at all?

6. Make a copy of a picture of you with your loved one. Paste it in your journal and write about the day that picture was taken.

7. Try writing in a spiral or a circle or diagonally across the page. Notice if this feels different.

8. Find quotes that move you, especially ones that help you cope. You might look up the word "resilience" on the internet and see what comes up, then write some of the more meaningful quotes in your journal. If you

9. Take your journal for a walk. Go to a pretty, pleasant place, take a deep breath before you start and walk very slowly, as if you are doing a walking meditation. Attune your senses to nature and notice sights, sounds, smells. Stop whenever you feel like you need to or want to. Sit down along your walk and just notice your surroundings. You can write how you feel or you can simply list what you notice. Later when you have finished your walk, you can write about how you felt before and afterwards. Remember to go slow and pay attention, both to what is happening in the natural world and what is happening in your own inner world.

10. Tell the story of your loss in your journal. Write as many details as you can, noticing how you feel as you tell your story. Is there an aspect of your emotional reaction to your story that you would like to shift? Can you write about that?

Nurturing yourself

Self-care and self-compassion are essential in difficult times. Practical strategies include tuning in to your own needs, nourishing your body, heart and soul, and writing down your feelings and thoughts.

Did you spend time as a caregiver for your loved one, tending to their needs and watching them decline due to illness? Did you put aside your own needs, including time for sleeping, eating and doing things for yourself so that you could remain at their side, hoping against hope for a rally back to health or a miracle to cure them? When you finally went to sleep, did you keep one part of your mind and heart focused on them in case they needed something?

If you did this, you most likely are exhausted. You may also feel jumpy and hyper-vigilant, even though they are gone now.

We are often unaccustomed to taking care of ourselves; in fact, some people are uncomfortable with the concept, as if they are not worthy of nurturing. Yet grieving is one of the hardest things you will ever do. If you don't take care of yourself, you won't be able to cope. If you don't get enough sleep, enough nutrition and enough down time, you might become ill.

In her book *Glad No Matter What*, Susan Ariel Rose Kennedy (SARK) points out that we need to apply "exquisite self-love and care especially during times of loss and change" (SARK, 2010, p.44). She goes on to say: "The subject of self-love is often misunderstood. It's usually thought of as egotistical or self-serving. In its purest and simple form, it is *you* loving *you* so that you can truly love others" (p.54). SARK goes on to suggest that we need to give ourselves "primary permission" to nurture and care for ourselves, especially when we are hurting. Instead of causing people to think badly of us when we do this, we might find ourselves in a better position to ask for help and support.

Take care of yourself by slowing down. If you are committed to doing something and it feels too hard, if at all possible, stop. Don't take on too much when you are grieving because it takes a huge amount of energy just to get through the day. Take lots of breaks. Take naps if you can fit them in, or just lie down and try to relax your body and mind for 10 minutes or so, even if you do not fall asleep. If you are working, you can still do this by finding a private place, closing the door, and lying down for a few minutes. Or, escape to the bathroom and sit in one of the stalls, just breathing.

If you are having trouble sleeping, try a soothing scent in your room. You can light a candle, infuse some essential oils into the air or simply put a drop of lavender or another calming oil on the soles of your feet, on your wrists and on your temples. Don't use too much and mix it with a carrier oil if your skin is sensitive. Lavender is particularly soothing, but some people don't like its smell. Be sure to use something that is pleasant and relaxing to you. There are also lotions that claim to be calming; perhaps they have a bit of essential oil in them or perhaps it is the mere suggestion that that they will calm you that does the trick! A hot bath with Epsom salts or bubbles in the evening before bed can also help you get more rest. If you are not sleeping and it is becoming a problem during the day, talk to your physician. Grieving takes a lot of mental and emotional energy; adequate rest is very important.

Drink calming and pleasant teas throughout the day. If you are fond of a certain kind, drink that, but I also recommend trying specific herbal teas that are soothing. Peppermint, licorice or ginger are nice. Chamomile or one of the calming or tension-relieving blends that can be found on supermarket shelves are helpful. You can even apply some self-nurturing by making a mindful cup of tea.

A mindful cup of tea

Making a cup of tea when you are stressed can be very helpful. There is a way to enhance the relaxing qualities of this activity by applying mindfulness.

- Choose a special cup for your tea. Choose a quiet, peaceful place to drink your tea, with a seat that is comfortable.

- Choose a tea that you really like—perhaps a relaxing kind like chamomile or peppermint. It doesn't matter what kind of tea you choose as long as it is something you like.

- Take a few deep breaths. Slowly fill the kettle. Listen to the sound of the water flowing into it. Turn on the flame and listen to its sound. Place the kettle on the flame to boil. Listen, smell, notice.

- Place your teabag in the tea cup. Notice the smell of the tea. If you like your tea with honey or sugar, lemon or milk, put this out now. Do everything slowly, noticing each action.

- Once the water boils, pour it over the tea. Smell the aromatic steam rising from the tea cup. Enhance your *tea in a way that is pleasing to you; steep it as long as you need, sweeten it or not.*

• *Now that your tea is ready, take a deep breath. Take the tea in its beautiful cup to your comfortable chair and sit down. Smell the tea, sip it slowly. Feel it enter your mouth, taste the tea. Let each moment of this activity be steeped in peace and serenity.*

Grief as trauma

Grief is a kind of trauma and the disruptive, unruly emotions associated with it are highly activating. This means that we find ourselves in a state of arousal, of primitive fight, flight or freeze modes. When you have suffered through the death of someone you care deeply about, there is often a fear that something else bad will happen. You may have been living your life in a relatively happy state, content in the knowledge that you knew what your goals were and what the shape of your life would be. Then, there was a diagnosis, or an accident or a sudden event that flipped you up into the air and shattered your world. In the moment of that hard crash, you learned a very uncomfortable fact. You are not in control of what happens.

As a person who believed that I could direct my life with the power of my mind and my intentions, this was indeed a very hard lesson, one that I did not particularly like. It caused some strange behaviors on my part as the lesson sank in. Three months after Alby died, our son totaled his sister's car and I stood in the middle of the street, yelling, "I get it! I have no control!" He was, by the way, completely unhurt except for a scratch on his forehead. The telephone pole was broken in half and the car was ruined, but he was safe. My body flooded with fear and trembling as the possibility of losing another family member stared me in the face.

The link between reactions to death and trauma are being studied now and there is some crossover. Trauma work relies heavily on working through the narrative of events, desensitizing the person to alleviate recurring flashbacks and triggers. When circumstances of the death are sudden, accidental or violent, the bereaved person often has flashbacks to the time of death or replays what happened when they found out. Certain sounds or smells trigger a burst of crying or a memory. Even when your person died after an illness and the terminality was known, some reactions similar to those found in trauma are present. When you find yourself startled by something seemingly small or are suddenly filled with a rush of fear that some other horrible event will happen, know that this is normal. Death and the changes it causes in your life are often traumatic. Understanding the connection helps you utilize techniques to cope. When you feel suddenly aroused by your grief or are experiencing an overreaction to something else, the first technique is to regulate your body to help yourself calm down. This can be accomplished easily by noticing your own breathing. Are you breathing fast? Is your breath shallow, more in your chest and throat than in your belly? Notice this.

Using your breath to help you relax is also a good way to care for yourself. In addition to helping quell a startle response, regulating your breath is beneficial after a big emotional release. If you are allowing yourself to cry when you need to, you may need to use your breath to calm down when you are done. Paying attention to your breath is a good way to do this.

Breathe to relax

Breath represents the ebb and flow of life, yet we usually pay no attention to the fact that we are breathing at this very moment. Focusing on the breath can help us relax and alleviate difficult emotions and troubled thoughts.

1. *Sit in a comfortable position. You can do this in an exposed place and it will work – you can do this breathing exercise on the subway, on a park bench or at your desk at work. Optimally, find a calm place where you will not be disturbed for a while. You can also do this exercise lying down.*

2. *Tune into your body. Notice where there is tension. Notice the temperature on your skin. Notice the fact that you are alive, you are breathing, you are here.*

3. *Focus on your breath. Notice how you breathe in, notice your exhalation.*

4. *Take a deep breath. Breathe in through your nose slowly, on a count of four.*

5. *Exhale slowly, on a count of six. Breathe out through your mouth. If you like, you can make a small sound as you breathe out – a whoosh sound or even a soft tone.*

6. *Repeat your slow inhalation and exhalation, allowing the outbreath to be longer than the in-breath.*

7. *When you inhale, think of this as deeply cleansing. Imagine air filling your lungs, permeating all the cells of your body. When you exhale, try to empty your lungs.*

8. *Imagine that the in-breath is drawing clear, loving energy into your body.*

9. *As you exhale, imagine that you are breathing out all distress.*

Seeking and finding support

Who offers help? Who is there for you? Where do you find support and safety?

Losing someone is bad enough but some people are bereft of others to help them. If this is the case, seek out a support group so you can connect with others in a similar situation. Hopefully, you have people who are there to support you. Those closest to you and to the person who died may also be experiencing loss; family members and friends also had a relationship with them and are mourning too. For this and for other reasons, you may find that the ones you thought would be the most supportive are not. You also may be surprised by someone who steps up, someone you did not expect to understand or to be there for you.

I was very lucky in this regard. I am the oldest of five siblings and my family, including their spouses, rallied around me. Friends flew in to be with us and many people called or visited.

Who supports you in your grief? Are they family members, friends or colleagues? Are you able to ask for help or for someone to just come and be with you? Notice who is available and who is not, and lean towards the ones who are more sympathetic.

Finding someone who can really listen to you as you share your story and your feelings can be very helpful, especially if they also knew and cared for the person you are mourning. When you share grief, you can help each other even though you all may grieve differently. This is partly due to the differences in relationship—a child grieves a parent in a different way than a sibling might. As you notice who supports you, can you also notice how you are aiding them in their grief?

Helping children grieve

While our own grief is hard enough, how can we help the children who may also be grieving the same person? It's important to understand that children experience and express their grief differently than adults and in many ways, take their cues from the adults in their lives.

Just as a baby develops over time, so does a child's response to their loss. We don't expect a six-month-old to speak in full sentences or be successful at playing baseball. In the same way, children under the age of six or seven can only understand what they are developmentally capable of. A young child has not developed the ability to think abstractly, so while they may weep when being told that someone they love died, they may also keep asking questions. Young children might say, "I know my uncle is dead, but is he going to come to my birthday party next summer?" They mean this seriously because they don't have a grasp on the permanence of death or even an abstract concept of time. Be patient when answering the questions of young children. It is wise to use real words such as "died" rather than "passed away," which is a euphemism that is harder to explain. Be careful when using the words "sick" or "ill" and explain it as different than that time a few months ago when the child had a fever. I once heard an anecdote about a four-year-old who kept begging his father for sugar water before he went to sleep. His father had told him that his grandfather had "run out of gas" and died. The little boy knew that sugar water made him burp so he thought that as long as he was burping, he would not, himself, run out of gas.

Parents often try to protect children from reality because they don't want them to be hurt. One family, whose mother was dying in hospice, told their children that grandma had gone on vacation. As grandma came close to dying, the mother did not know what to tell them now that Grandma was not going to come back from Florida. While she told this falsehood to spare her children distress, she realized that now that her mother would be gone for good, she would have to cause them more hurt by admitting that she had lied.

This impulse is a loving one but sometimes it also comes from the fact that the adult simply doesn't know how to explain it, is hurting themselves and doesn't want or know how to deal with the child's questions. Parents and grandparents worry that including a child in funeral rites would be too difficult for the child. The opposite is true. A child who is included might cry and be sad but this child will also have an opportunity to say goodbye, express their own feelings and participate in the rituals of their family.

When things are not explained in age-appropriate, clear language to a child, the child imagines all kinds of scenarios, some of them worse than reality. Since young children do not have the emotional language to express themselves, their confusion and discomfort will come out in their behavior. While this is also true when they are included, some of the fantasizing and how they resolve incorrect information can be alleviated when the adults in their lives are willing to listen, allow them to express their sorrow in their own way and help them through it.

When I work with young clients, they often come to me with a referral from the school, which is concerned that the child is "not concentrating" or is having behavior issues. While teachers and school officials understand that there has been a death, they also seem to think that a child, even one as young as four, should be talking about their grief. These professionals are genuinely concerned about the child but they often apply their ideas of what adult grief ought to look like, expecting the child to cry for a while, then go about living normally. With young children, the reactions are subtler. Sometimes behavioral issues are related to the death, and other times they are simply an offshoot of development.

Dr. Phyllis Silverman and Dr. William Worden, both experienced grief therapists and researchers, conducted a longitudinal study at Harvard University to discover how children and adolescents grieve. Dr. Silverman described their findings in an article entitled *Living with Grief: Children, Adolescents and Loss* (Silverman, 2017). The Harvard Child Bereavement Study reinforced the fact that children and teens often experience a delay in their grief reactions. Sometimes it can take up to two years for a child or adolescent to express their feelings about their loss. Young children often do not talk about their loss other than to state clearly who died and how it happened, sometimes at odd moments like on the playground in casual conversation with another child. Publicly, they do not necessarily weep or exhibit strong emotion. Adults might worry that they are "not grieving" and also have to deal with the fall-out for others when the child suddenly blurts out information. In the case of a father's suicide, a child might turn to another on a swing and say in a matter of fact way, "My Daddy killed himself." The parent then gets a phone call from school and has to cope with other parents who might be sympathetic or might not.

This is how a child expresses grief. They are having trouble understanding the finality of it and tell the story. One little girl skipped into my office, turned herself upside down in the chair and commented, "My mommy died." I agreed and told her it was sad. "Can we make a picture now?" she asked. We moved over to the drawing table and drew pictures. When I asked her if she'd like to draw one for her mom, she agreed but she didn't say anything related to her loss for the rest of the session.

Children may have difficulty using words to express the upheaval in their lives when a parent, grandparent or sibling dies. But they might have nightmares that they cannot remember or have trouble sleeping alone or in the dark. They might have trouble going to school; or if they do go, staying there for a full day. Their grief follows their emotional development and we would be wise to allow them to grieve at their own pace.

Children from six or seven through pre-teens are beginning to think abstractly and these children can become very worried after a death. They realize that it could happen to someone else and may fear that this could happen to the surviving adults. Who will care for them if someone else dies? They also are now aware that death can happen to anyone, at any age. They need to be heard, to be guided towards expressing their unique feelings. Any of the creative techniques in this book will also work with children and teens.

Pre-teens and early adolescents as well as children of all ages need to feel that life will go on. They need to know that it is important to continue to grow, to have friends, to try new things. It would be helpful for their caregivers to be open to them, to let them know that there is someone who will listen if they want to talk without pressuring them to do so.

Children learn by observing. If adults suppress and hide their own grief, children learn that it is not acceptable to express how they feel. I felt strongly that one of my jobs as a grieving parent was to model how to get through it. I did not allow my teenage children to witness my complete breakdowns very often, but they did see some of them. They were aware that I was weeping in the shower. They witnessed how hard it was for me to get through the day; and while it was frightening for them at times, I sought to reassure them that we were all capable of surviving. In the midst of that seeming inability to function, I also made sure that we went to concerts or shows, that they continued to hang out with their friends, go to school, engage in life.

In fact, my commitment to honoring and releasing my emotions, coupled with a focus on continuing to engage in some degree of normal life, helped my teenaged children see that we have the ability to endure catastrophe. We can spend time sobbing with abandon and then we can pick ourselves up and go to the prom. While I was modeling re-engaging in life in the midst of my own collapse, I also learned how to honor grief, to welcome its extremely divisive and unsettling presence into my home as I struggled to figure out how to cope with it.

One early thought was that even as I had trouble truly accepting that he was dead, I knew that I was alive. I did not know how I would live or what I would do. But I knew that I would find my way through the jagged stumps in the landscape of my life. I knew that I would plant new trees and discover new territories, once the agony subsided. It was clear that this would take some time.

All of us—no matter what age we are—will probably experience reactions when important life events happen, major achievements that shape the lives of our family. For me, graduations, weddings and the upcoming births of grandchildren are both filled with joy and sadness as each one is yet another thing where Alby is not here. What changes as the years go by is that the extreme sorrow slowly transmutes into a more manageable sense of wistfulness. Longing for him, feeling it is so unfair and wrong that he is not here has shifted into a sense that he, too, is missing our milestones.

Do you have a friend or two who is willing to come over and just be with you, take a walk or have a cup of tea and listen? Call them up and ask them. If they are busy, ask them to commit to a different time.

Creating meaningful rituals

Simple rituals such as lighting a candle, setting a place for your dead loved one or placing a flower in front of a photograph can be helpful in grounding grief and relating to your loved one after they die.

Humans have always created rituals to explain what cannot be explained and to create a container for the emotions that arise. Funeral rites express the religious beliefs of the loved one and of the family. Prayers, hymns and other songs, and eulogies which honor the person who has died are all ways in which we gather people together to mourn and to help each other heal. Some religions have 40 days of specific prayers to help the dying soul on its way to the afterlife. Others have a period of mourning when the family sits on wooden boxes and receives guests who bring food and comfort, joining in rounds of prayer at specific times.

The initial time after a death is usually taken up with the rituals of family, religion and community. These are shaped by our culture and spiritual beliefs, providing a framework for "how" to grieve, at least in those few weeks. There are arrangements to be made and often people to help you take care of them. Important decisions are made in those first hours. How will you tell people about the death? Who would you like to have around you at this time? Which funeral home? Will you have a burial or cremation? Will there be viewing or receiving hours and a service of some kind, and where? How do you write an obituary?

The rituals surrounding death give friends and family a chance to come together to share in the grief. These are more for the living than for the dead and we often feel supported by the presence of others, even as we feel like we can't stand up. Rituals provide comfort for us with remembrances, eulogies, music and food. Sometimes we do them because they are expected or because they will help some of the others who have also lost this person.

Gathering for the funeral provides support, a forum to share sorrow and stories about the person who died. But after these rituals are over, everyone else returns to ordinary life. The family members are left with their intense grief, which, as the numbness wears off, seems to increase over time. Creating some other rituals can be very helpful.

RITUALS AT THE TIME OF DEATH

If you are present at the death, there may be opportunity to take a few moments (or however long you need) for a final ritual. When I worked in a hospice, it was customary to give the family time alone with their family member, to say goodbye or to sit at the bedside and weep. We offered gentle support, cups of water and tissues, and privacy.

If you are not there, you can still create a ritual of saying a final goodbye. Find a nice photograph of the person and speak to it as if you are speaking to them. You can do this privately so that you feel free to say whatever is in your heart.

One sticky issue for people after a death is whether they were present at that last moment or not. Some people long to be there, not wanting their loved one to be alone. When I worked in a hospice, one common observation of the staff was that it seemed that the dying person would either wait for family members to arrive before dying or they would wait for family members to leave the room. This was often a shock to the person who just went out to get a glass of water and now feels like they "missed" the death. They worry that they were not able to provide comfort in those last moments.

It was a common discussion in the halls of the hospice. It appears that there is some choice on the part of the person who is dying and it seems that if they waited for their caregivers to leave, it might be because they wanted to spare them those last moments. I see it as an act of kindness, however it turned out. If they waited for everyone to gather, that was very kind of them. And if they waited for them to leave the room, they probably were also offering one last instant of kindness. If this happened to you, accept, if you can, that it happened as it was supposed to and that you did the best you could.

RITUALS FOR SPECIAL DAYS

After someone dies, special days can be hard to handle. What will you do on the first anniversary of their death? How about their birthday, Father's Day or Mother's Day? Was there a special day you celebrated with them and now are at a loss to figure out what to do?

Special days often loom menacingly before they arrive, causing a lot of anxiety. Head this off by developing a plan to connect with your loved one, or to treat yourself well so that you can get through this difficult day.

Creating a small ritual to honor them on a special day can help. It could be as simple as finding a lovely place to walk, especially if they enjoyed nature. You can imagine that you are taking them with you, metaphorically or spiritually. Some people like to involve other people and some prefer to do this alone or with a chosen few. Enjoying a meal that they would have liked, spending time with people you love and telling a story or two to remember them can also get you through a special day.

MAKE A SHRINE

In many Asian cultures it is customary to place a large photograph of the deceased on a table, surrounded by candles, flowers, incense and even food. You may have photographs of your loved one in many places in your home. Would it be helpful to you to establish one special spot where you can create a ritual on a daily basis?

Choose a shelf or a table and place a special picture of your loved one on it. Add objects that were meaningful to them, or perhaps are meaningful to your relationship. Did they have a favorite color? Perhaps you can place a piece of fabric in this color on the surface, under the photo. Add any items you like—a vase that can be filled with a single flower or a bouquet or even a small potted plant. Place a stone or a piece of jewelry on the shelf, if that feels right for you. If you add candles, this could be part of the ritual you create. If you like, you can "visit" this little shrine every day to say hello to your loved one. Light a candle as a way of connecting. Make sure any flowers are fresh and change them when you need to.

This kind of ritual can be very personal and does not need any other participants. It creates a way of remembering and a way of connecting.

VISITING THE CEMETERY

For many people, visiting the cemetery is a meaningful way to connect. Tending the grave, placing flowers or planting them on or near the grave are ways of tending to a loved one after they die. Some people sit and talk, sharing aspects of their daily lives. Some bring a chair and read a book, imagining that they are spending time with them. Placing a stone on the marker is a symbolic way of letting them know you were there. Whatever you do if you visit the resting place, remember that this is also a ritual of connection and remembrance.

Not everyone has a grave site to visit nor is it meaningful to them to do so. You can establish your own special place by planting a tree in your garden or installing a special bench. You might create a mosaic remembrance tile and lay it somewhere special in your yard.

If your loved one was cremated, you might develop a ritual around spreading ashes. If this feels right, think about where and when you would like to do this. Think about who you would like to have with you. If you wish, bring something you wrote or a poem or quote that moves you. Take your time. Releasing the ashes of your loved one is not easy.

Alby and I had talked about our wishes and had decided that we did not want to be buried but would prefer cremation. Since he was so young when he died, we did not continue this conversation so I had no idea where he would want his ashes scattered. I thought that, since he was so engaged in the world, he might like to be taken all over it, but I kept my thoughts to myself.

Around the first anniversary, I sat my children down and asked them what they imagined. They thought briefly and then said, "He should be taken to many places." So it was clear that we agreed.

I purchased a large urn with six smaller matching ones. Alone in my room, I lined them all up and placed the black box from the funeral home before me. I had a moment of fear as I opened the box, then shock as I viewed the contents. I will not describe them to you here, other than to say that I was surprised by the appearance. The idea that this was all that was left of him was also shocking. Taking a deep breath, I slowly distributed his ashes into the seven urns. Three of the smaller ones went to his mother, his sister and his brother, and I have the other three in a velvet box, one for each of our children. Perhaps someday they will ask for theirs.

After the initial scattering in the center of the garden at our home, I took some of his ashes whenever I traveled. I visited places that were meaningful to him and released him there. I went to places that we had traveled to together and places that neither of us had ever been. Since I thought he would have liked to visit Thailand, India and Nepal, I took him along. I took his ashes to France; I took him to lakes and to the sea. Finally, I returned to the beach in Connecticut where he had spent all his childhood summers. At sunrise, I walked out on a jetty and released his ashes one final time.

WRITE A LETTER

Many clients talk about how they didn't get to say certain things to their loved one before they died. I believe that you can still talk to them and say what you need to say. It is fine to talk to them out loud; a lot of people do this on a regular basis, some looking over their shoulder to make sure no one thinks they are nuts. You are not crazy to talk to your dear one; you miss them and you miss that conversation. Go ahead and talk if it feels right.

You also might write them a letter, telling them the things you wish you had said. You can use this letter as an opportunity to thank them for the gift of their life, let them know how they have influenced you. Your letter might also say how you will continue their legacy and what that means to you. Or you just might write a letter that says, "Hello. I miss you so much."

"Corresponding with the deceased" is the name of a chapter in one of my grief therapy resource books and is a proven technique to help you remain connected. Robert Neimeyer says that this is a way to address what has not been spoken but also to reconnect: "The most therapeutic letters appear to be those in which the griever speaks deeply from the heart about what is important as he or she attempts to *reopen* contact with the deceased, rather than seek 'closure' of the relationship" (Neimeyer, 2012a, p.259)

A personal journal is a good place in which to write letters, or you might keep a special container to hold them. Messages can be put on small pieces of paper, placed in a box and left on the gravesite. The point is we can still communicate with our loved ones after they die and it is actually beneficial to do so.

Writing a letter is a good way for children to connect with someone who has died. Young children might draw a picture for their father or for their grandmother. Letters can be placed on a personal shrine or put in a memory box, or brought to the grave site. Some people have even burned letters (in a safe container and outside, of course!) and imagined their words going up to heaven with the smoke.

It is important to remember that when you create a ritual for yourself there are no rules that can be broken. Follow your heart and let it lead you to where you feel connected to the person who has died. Then create something that is meaningful to you and would also have been meaningful to them.

BEING IN NATURE

Alby was a very outdoorsy kind of guy. He loved to dig holes in the ground and plant things in them. He built stone walls and walkways. The early morning would call him outside and he would wander slowly on the lawn, among the trees, staring up at the sky or down at the ground where plants and flowers were growing. He would pick a leaf, crush it in his fingers and inhale its scent.

Part of my own healing process involved taking long walks. I felt connected to him when I was outside. Even though it often made me cry in the beginning, I would walk slowly, sometimes pausing to admire a flower or stopping to notice a bunny hopping on the trail up ahead. A feather caught in a bramble would become a treasure to bring home.

Walking in nature can actually become a kind of meditation. There is a practice in Japan called "Shinrinn-Yoku," which means forest bathing. The idea is to walk in a forest or in nature slowly, to absorb the scents and atmosphere as a way of connecting to the earth and breathe in the healthful plant essences. Becoming aware of your surroundings and noticing what is all around becomes an exercise in patience, in quietude. Slow down your pace when you walk, tuning your senses to the sounds of leaves rustling or small animals in the underbrush. Feel your feet as they touch the ground, becoming aware of the shape of the terrain. Bathe in nature. If you like, you might bring along a small journal and a pen. At some point in your "forest bath," sit down beneath a tree or on a stone. Write about what you notice, how you feel. When you are ready, continue on your way.

Slowing down

Our quick-fix culture demands that we "get over" things rapidly. Slowing down and honoring the process is a better way. If you give yourself time to grieve, the healing will actually be accomplished sooner than if you push it away and ignore it. Also, slowing down to immerse yourself in nature, in art, music, poetry and movement, encourages engagement in new things.

When you are grieving, time feels different, as if you are moving through mud. Instead of fighting this odd sensation, why not give yourself permission to slow down? While friends, bosses and the outside world might pressure you to get back to "normal," deep in your core you know this is impossible. Why not take the time you need?

No one can say how long it will take to recover after the death of a loved one, because each person is different. There are so many factors that impact reactions, including the type of relationship, the type of death, and what your history of loss experiences might be. No one should tell you that you must "complete" your bereavement in a certain amount of time. Since you don't know, can you allow yourself to be comfortable with not knowing? In reality, there is not actual recovery from grief; there is only repair and figuring out how to construct your life on the other side of it.

By giving yourself permission to engage in and experience your own personal reactions to death, you might very well find that this path through grief will lead you towards healing of some kind. By expressing and releasing your emotions, you will be better able to digest them and soften their rawness. There is no way around, although you might try distractions, travel, keeping busy and trying not to think. Ultimately, these diversions don't really hold.

Another aspect of slowing down in order to heal is that you can engage in activities that help you relax. Reading may be difficult due to concentration issues, but if that is a problem, you might try reading poetry or short stories. Watching movies or listening to music can be relaxing even if they contribute to sad feelings.

MINDFULNESS AND SIMPLE MEDITATION

Mindful meditation is a simple form of quieting the mind and body. While it has its roots in religious practice, what I recommend is not religious in any way. Many people engage in yoga as a form of exercise coupled with releasing stress and ruminating thoughts, and yoga, too, has its religious roots. Yet the majority of the yoga studios in the West are not promoting any religion; rather they offer ways to increase physical health through stretching and strengthening the body, as well as using breath and some imagery to calm the mind.

Mindfulness is simply a way of paying attention. Sitting in one position, usually with legs crossed and back straight but not tense, you can practice mindfulness by paying attention to your breath. Notice your inhalation and your exhalation. Slow it down. Notice that you are still thinking but allow your thoughts to float away and just concentrate on your breath, in a gentle, quiet manner.

Some people do this while sitting in a chair, feet flat on the floor. This can be more comfortable for some and this is an important factor if you want to engage in a relatively successful mindfulness exercise. I like to sit on a cushion, and instead of crossing my legs, I tuck my knees on either side of the cushion with my lower legs pointing back, as if I were kneeling. Because I am on a cushion there is no pressure on my knees and this position allows me to sit upright for a longer period of time without any cramps. It is also okay to do a mindful meditation while lying down.

Some people find that focusing on a candle, a flower or even making a simple sound helps them concentrate. Some even have a mantra that they repeat. Try different things to see what works. There are a lot of resources in libraries or online that can help you. Natural sounds like ocean or rain are also useful when you are first trying a relaxing meditation.

Again, the focus is on simply being, sitting with your breath, experiencing what is. Of course, when we are grieving, this is very difficult to do since we are quite unhappy about what is. But sitting calmly, reducing the number of intrusive thoughts and just being still for a while is a good practice. Being mindful means to notice what is and to not try to change it.

When I first tried to "meditate," I thought I had to do it a certain way and spent most of the period of time noticing how I was not doing it "correctly." Part of the problem was that my hips cramped up in a cross-legged position. Another part of the issue was that the leader started the meditation with these instructions:

"Still your mind."

I obediently crossed my legs, tried to stop thinking and immediately burst into tears. I did so very, very quietly so as not to disturb the others in the room who, obviously, had this meditation thing down. I was so out of tune with everyone, obviously doing it in the wrong way, so unable to comply with the task that I felt devastated almost immediately. My hips hurt, my foot fell asleep and I was crying! Of course, this was only a few months after the death, so nearly everything that did not happen in a completely smooth manner threw me into a fit. On top of it all, I had neglected to bring tissues.

What I learned later, and what I finally accept, is that it is nearly impossible to stop thinking. The mind will not stop, but we don't have to be so involved in our thoughts all the time. One way around this when you are trying to sit in mindfulness is to let go of the attachment to the thought that arises. Imagine that the thought is like a fast-moving cloud in the sky of your mind; it arises and floats off towards the horizon. Another rises and off it goes. Meanwhile, focus just on your breath. As you follow your breath, you are also engaging with the present moment—being here right now, as you sit, not worrying about how you will handle tomorrow or what you will make for dinner or why you are so sad, lonely or angry. If those thoughts come up, let them float away and just sit, within the moment, within the movement of your breath.

Slowing down as part of nurturing yourself also includes being kind. Therefore, if I sit in a mindful meditation and I am unable to stop being engaged in my thoughts, I just focus on sitting quietly. I allow myself to think without letting the thoughts distress me. When this happens, my "mantra" is this: "It's my meditation and I'll think if I want to!"

When you become a little more adept, it is possible to sometimes achieve a heightened sense of integration and focus. For me, it feels as if I drop into a quiet spaciousness and my thoughts really recede. I no longer have to remind myself to focus on anything; I am able to simply *be*. When this happens, I feel as if I have touched a deeper way of being, at least for a few moments. And I find that when I am able to touch this space, even if only for a few minutes, I do feel less anxious and little more regulated in my emotions. And as long as I am not criticizing myself, I am slowly getting better at it.

Sitting still is not natural for me. I have been a dancer all my life and moving is what I do. Walking meditations are another way to come in to a sense of mindfulness and it is a practice that works very well for me. I often choose two points or even two trees and walk slowly around them. Sometimes I create points by placing a stone on the ground, and if it is not windy, I can place a candle on the stone. You can even set up a meaningful pattern on the ground if you like; spirals are very organic and there is a metaphor inherent in them as you move in to the center then circle back out again. Labyrinths are constructed for meditative purposes, so if you are fortunate enough to have one near you, try a moving meditation in a labyrinth and see how it feels.

Before you start your walking meditation, center yourself and, if you like, state an intention or ask a question. Stretch your arms up to the sky, take a deep breath and lower your arms, then your head, neck, shoulders and eventually your back until you are bent over towards the ground. Don't push this; go only as low as is comfortable without hindering your breath or causing pain. If it feels right, you can swing around or shake out your arms, your legs, your head. When you are ready, take a deep breath and slowly rise to reach your arms up again. Repeat this several times to ground yourself and clear out any energy that is holding you back. Then, when you are ready, enter your walking meditation.

You can walk in a straight line around the two points or you can weave an infinity shape. Continue to breathe and walk slowly. If you have set an intention, keep a gentle focus on it. Don't try too hard. Walk until you feel you've had enough. Then do the grounding stretch again to close your meditation.

CHAPTER 4

Opening to Emotion

The emotions of grief take a lot of energy as you figure out how to cope. While there might be a tendency to try to control emotions, grief becomes easier to manage when feelings are expressed. The metaphors of mourning sometimes provide clues to help us. This is scary and I recommended a timed release of genuine emotion, as if you were dosing yourself with it. This chapter also normalizes the broad spectrum of grief reactions commonly felt by people while recognizing that each person is unique as is their grief.

Bereavement, grief and mourning are very much about emotion. Your personality, the circumstances of the death, who the person was to you and what kind of relationship you had, and even your family history of dealing with crisis and loss, will influence how you experience and express these feelings.

One of the crazy aspects of loss is how extreme and erratic these emotions can be. You may feel deep sadness in one moment then flip into rage the next. You might feel depressed, nervous and lost, all at the same time. Perhaps you considered yourself strong and competent prior to the death but now you are filled with a sense that something terrible could happen at any minute. Now that you know tragedy, you are almost certain that another terrible event will happen in the next moment.

Actually, I thought I was losing my mind. I could not concentrate; I could not read more than a sentence or two at a time unless it was a very short book about coping with death. I forgot what I was doing and had to keep extensive lists in order to remember to pay bills, buy groceries, etc. My emotions were so fluid and changeable that I feared for my mental health.

C.S. Lewis, author of *The Chronicles of Narnia*, *The Screwtape Letters* and other books, wrote a slim volume about the death of his wife and his process of dealing with it. It is called *A Grief Observed* and begins with this:

No one ever told me that grief felt so like fear. I am not afraid, but the sensation is like being afraid. The same fluttering in the stomach, the same restlessness, the same yawning. I keep on swallowing.

At other times it feels like being drunk or mildly concussed. There is a sort of invisible blanket between the world and me. I find it hard to take in what anybody says. Or perhaps, hard to want to take it in..." (Lewis, 1961, p.16)

I read this and thought, "Oh. Yes. This is exactly how I feel. I am not mentally ill; it just feels that way. And I have never been so terrified in my life, but I now can see that this is a symptom of my grief." While recognizing this did not quell my emotions, at least I understood that they had a reason for being as insanely volatile as they were.

I always considered myself comfortable with my emotions and, as many people in my life can testify, they have always been quite strong. What was surprising to me was that I suddenly felt very private within my bereavement. It was so enormous, so overwhelming, that I did not want it to spill out all over the place. I needed a container, a safe space in which to collapse. Of course, the waves of sadness crashed over me at strange times, such as: on line at the bank or just saying hello to an acquaintance at the post office. This was extremely uncomfortable and, for a person who thought she had emotional expression locked down, it was disheartening.

There were days that felt like molasses when everything seemed to move so slowly. These days were very difficult because it felt like they would never end. There were days that seemed to disappear, and I would get to the evening and have no idea what had happened. I was confused and unsettled. I wrote:

> *Rocky past two weeks – frankly I am miserable. I feel so…*
> *small, ordinary, unspecial. I feel*
> *guilty, I feel unbalanced, lost,*
> *overwhelmed, ugly, sad,*
> *angry and alone, abandoned*
> *and alone.*

Out of place in a suddenly uncomfortable
life that is twisted around.
I still can't grasp this sudden turn
This absolute
HALT.

~ (PERSONAL JOURNAL, FEBRUARY 2006)

In my past iterations as a musician, I had learned to use emotions to inform a song in order to connect with an audience. As a choreographer, I used emotion and gesture to demonstrate relationships between people. As a writer, emotions were spilled into my teenage journals in the form of poetry, so I was no stranger to delving into my feelings and giving them voice. I intuitively knew that in order to get to the other side of this horrible, suddenly widowed condition, it would be better to plunge in than to try to avoid this giant pool of messy sensations and reactions. I needed to feel it all.

At the same time, it would have been impossible to stay in that state of heightened agitation all the time. And it really is scary; there is a sense that if you completely break down, you may never get up again. One approach to this problem is to titrate your breakdown: in other words, allow yourself a dose of completely letting go, but time it so that you will know when to climb back out.

When you feel a breakdown coming on, first notice if you are in a safe place where you might be free to let it out. If you are, allow yourself a certain amount of time, such as 5–10 minutes. Give in to your meltdown and let it out. I always found myself on the floor when this happened, so allow your body to give in to what it needs as you rail at the universe, cry, moan, scream—whatever you need. Keep aware of the time though, because as you get closer to the time limit you set for yourself, you need to start to take some deep breaths to calm yourself down. Wrap your arms around yourself. Breathe. When you are ready, slowly get up, wipe your face and blow your nose. Splash some cold water on your face. When you feel calmer, notice that this emotional release, as extreme as it might have been, was good for you. Congratulate yourself.

Releasing emotion creatively

The body is the first responder to emotion. Often we can sense disturbances within our bodies before we even recognize a strong feeling. It may appear as a perception of icy cold in the belly or a fluttering sensation presaging a wave of grief. As I moved into the first months of grief, I began to notice myself wringing my hands and rubbing my forehead. I would do this unconsciously but when I became aware of it, I noticed that it happened just before a breakdown.

By paying attention to what was happening in my body—the movements I was unconsciously making—I was able to make a choice. I could look around and see if I was in a safe place. If I was at home, I could allow myself to melt into a puddle of sorrow. If I was out in public, I could find a bathroom or a quiet place. By listening to the signals from my body, I had a little time in which to pull myself together if there was no place to retreat to.

What happens in your body when emotions well up? Take an inventory if you can; notice the sensations that happen just before you are bowled over by a grief wave.

In my Master's program, there was an assignment that was designed to explore the physical sensations of emotion. This is a technique that can help identify, soothe and release them, using an expressive art technique.

Releasing in color

To creatively release emotion, you are going to draw the feeling inside your body. Don't worry about what it looks like; this exercise is all about how it feels.

You will need some paper and some oil or chalk pastels. I usually like to have some paper towels nearby to help me rub the colors together if that feels right.

Lay out your materials and take a deep breath. Tune into your body and notice any sensations within.

Pick a color that corresponds to the feeling. Without looking at the paper, draw the sensation. Use more than one color if you wish.

According to psychologist Alan Wolfelt:

You cannot heal without mourning or expressing your grief outwardly. Denying your grief, running from it, or minimizing it only seems to make it more confusing and overwhelming. To lessen your hurt, you must embrace it. As strange as it may seem, you must make it your friend. (Wolfelt, 2003, p.15)

Sorrow

Death is an ending and therefore, we react to it with sadness. Sorrow makes us cry; it feels depressing and overwhelming. Sadness is often very wet, so metaphors of drowning in it capture something of the experience.

Tears are important because they help us release sadness. Kübler-Ross called them "one of our many wondrous built-in healing mechanisms" (Kübler-Ross and Kessler, 2005, p.42). The breakdown of sorrow provides an outlet for emotion and we generally feel better for a while after a good cry. In addition, physicians have discovered that tears relieve stress, allowing the body to purge what is bottled up so that these feelings don't turn into physical pain and dis-ease. We produce three kinds of tears: One type continuously lubricates the eyes, keeping membranes moist. Another type floods our eyes to clear out any irritating particles. Emotional tears are different and, according to researchers such as Dr. William Frey (as discussed in Orloff, 2010), they actually excrete toxins and stimulate the production of endorphins. This means that allowing your sorrow to spill out of your eyes in the form of tears is healthy, releasing both emotion and accumulated stress hormones, allowing us to heal. Psychologist Judith Orloff says:

> Crying is also essential to resolve grief, when waves of tears periodically come over us after we experience a loss. Tears help us process the loss so we can keep living with open hearts. Otherwise, we are a set up for depression if we suppress these potent feelings. (Orloff, 2010)

We often believe that the breakdown of sorrow shows us to be weak. This false belief is promoted by people we encounter who exhort us to be strong in the face of grief. In my opinion, strength is highly overrated, especially in early grief; when we are overwhelmed by loss and sorrow, we have no choice but to express it and crying is a really good way to do this. Wolfelt advises that it is important "to not be ashamed of your tears and profound feelings of sadness" (Wolfelt, 2003, p.15). He reminds us that our sorrow is rooted in love and needs to be felt and expressed.

How is showing your feelings weakness, especially when it is so hard to let it out? I would suggest that allowing yourself to be vulnerable enough to fall on the floor and sob is actually a strength in itself. Allowing yourself this important expressive release is also healthy.

Of course there are times when crying is not appropriate, but you can make time for yourself to let go. When you are in a safe place, either alone or with a safe, supportive person, don't suppress your sadness. Allow it to rise from your heart to the surface of your eyes, spilling out over your cheeks. Allow sorrow to fill your body and seep out of your pores. Spend some time mourning what you have lost; it is a necessary part of grief and will torment you if you try to hold it back or ignore it.

Most of the time, sorrow is connected to love. If we did not love, we would not mourn. Smile in the midst of sadness as you remember this love.

Anger

Anger is an emotion that has a bad reputation. It is often socially unacceptable to express it because we can say things in anger that we might regret later. Anger can be hurtful both to the people at which it is directed and also to ourselves.

But anger has some positive benefits as well. The poet May Sarton called it "buried fire" (Sarton, 2010, p.29) and it can be a motivator to stimulate action. Anger can also be a fuel, a catalyst for change, especially in cases of injustice. Anger is a natural response to loss and it is healthier to let it rise up, express it constructively if possible and then work to dissipate it.

Kübler-Ross identified anger as one of the basic stages of grief which is often one of the first reactions to death, part of the sense of disbelief and unfairness created by loss. Some anger is justified when someone dies. We might be angry that the doctors did not diagnose the disease soon enough. We might be angry at the person who died, because they did not take care of themselves or had a bad habit that contributed to, or even caused, their death. If there was an accident, we could be very angry at the circumstances of this tragedy as well as at the people who appear to have been at fault. The cause of our suffering (the death itself) is reason enough to be angry.

Kübler-Ross points out that anger has a protective quality in that it serves as a shell over other, deeper feelings that we might not be ready to lean into. She labeled it as a stage because she felt it was such an important part of the healing process. It is also an easier emotion to express than sadness.

...anger is the emotion we are most used to managing. We often choose it to avoid the feelings underneath until we are ready to face them. It may feel all-consuming, but as long as it doesn't consume you for a long period of time, it is part of your emotional management. It is a useful emotion until you have moved past the first waves of it. Then you will be ready to go deeper. (Kübler-Ross and Kessler, 2005, p.12)

You have every right to feel angry, if that is the emotion that arises. You have every right to explore the reasons you are angry, and to engage in some healthy expression. Find a way to release your anger rather than unleash it. Perhaps you are frustrated that you were not able to prevent the death, or are suffering from a sense of being abandoned. It may not be so effective to direct your anger towards any one particular person but if there is someone who is at fault in your eyes, you could write a letter to them. Write a letter expressing how you feel, how angry you are, what you feel they did to cause the situation. The trick here is to do this in order to help yourself; in other words, write the letter but do not send it. Write the letter in your journal. Or write it on paper, long hand, then find a way to release it—both the story, the emotion and the actual words. You might make a small, contained fire and once you have read your letter (preferably out loud) you can toss it in the fire and watch your anger burn. You might tear it into little pieces after reading it and throw it into the wind or into a stream, river or into the ocean. However, you choose to release it, anger needs to have its say. As psychologist William Worden points out, "If anger is not adequately acknowledged, it can lead to complicated mourning" (Worden, 2009, p.19).

There is another way to cope with anger, besides identifying and expressing how it makes you feel. I often think that anger is a secondary emotion masquerading as a primary one because it is flashy and easy to vent. It is easier to be angry than to really feel all the pain associated with the loss of your loved one. This is a good thing initially because it gives us the opportunity of venting emotional energy with anger and rage until we are better equipped to engage in sorrow. Another coping mechanism is to see your anger as it arises and then take a deep breath in the midst of the feeling. Imagine your anger is a particular part of you and has an important message for you. Take another breath. Ask your anger what it is trying to tell you. At first it might say something like,

"I am sooooo furious that she died!"

Offer a little thanks to your anger for such a clear message. Then ask, "What is behind that?" Anger might say,

"I feel lost."

Or "I feel so helpless."

Or "I feel so alone."

The acknowledgment or gratitude for the message anger is trying to give you is important because it gives anger a voice. Once it has had its say, and you have heard it, you can move on. Now you have moved beyond your anger into the realm of the emotions that are hiding behind its flashiness. This enables you to make a choice on how to deal with these emotions. You can choose to express your anger and release it by venting it, either to someone or on a page in your journal. Or you might ask yourself if you are ready to delve tentatively into those feelings of helplessness, loneliness and abandonment that often are grief's escorts.

Another technique that can be effective when anger flares up is to ask yourself if it is helpful for you to feel this angry. You may be very angry that the person died, yet continuing to be involved with this anger will not bring them back. If anger is energy, can you shift some of this energy towards coping with other, deeper reactions to this death?

Moving feelings

Close your eyes. Feel your anger rise up within you. Notice where it is locating within your body. Put your hand on that part of your body. Breathe. Feel your anger rise up.

Pay attention to the quality of your anger, its energy. See if it is moving around and move your hand with it. Allow its energy to buzz to shake within you, and let it travel out through your arms, to your fingertips. As the energy travels through your arms, shake them. Swing your arms gently around your center, moving the energy of anger from inside your body to outside. Shake it out. Breathe while you vigorously shake your anger around, vibrating it through your body. Bend your knees one at a time so *the energy doesn't get stuck in your legs. Move your torso around, bending forward a bit, arching a bit, tipping from side to side. Don't force any movement but continue to shake, wriggle and swing anger through your body.*

Imagine as you move the energy of anger around that you are expelling it. Shake it out, toss it out of your body. When you feel you have released a lot of it, reach both your arms up to the sky. Take a deep breath. With a big exhale, drop your arms and swing them back, following this movement with your torso. Bend your knees. Take a deep breath and swing back up, reaching your arms to the sky. Swing back and forth, using your breath to cleanse anger out of your body. Then stand still, in a comfortable position. Notice your breath. Inhale. Exhale. Notice if you feel calmer.

Go get a drink of water.

Numbness

There is often a sense of shock when someone dies, and this cuts off feeling. Just as anger can be protective, an outward expression of emotion that keeps sorrow at bay, numbness is another coping emotion which gives us a little time to absorb what has happened. Numbing or shutting down provides a little space in which to learn to cope. Worden says that numbness "probably occurs because there are so many feelings to deal with that to allow them all into consciousness would be overwhelming, so the person experiences numbness as a protection from this flood of feelings" (Worden, 2009, p.23).

Numbness can be frightening because we think we "should" be feeling something. Instead, we might feel foggy, disconnected, unnervingly quiet and spacey. Not only is this strange but it can be a little frightening, especially if we have spent hours crying and suddenly, seemingly, feel nothing. The reverse of this is possible too; some people feel anaesthetized in the beginning and don't cry at all. This also causes worry, as if by not crying, they did not care.

It's important to remember that we all have a tendency to question our emotions and whether we are grieving "properly." If you notice this tendency in yourself, please let it go. Whatever you are feeling, even if it is numbing nothingness, is temporary, impermanent and perfectly okay.

Fear and anxiety

When someone close to us dies, someone intrinsically a part of our lives, it can make us feel unsafe. We often have an expectation of stability and a certain shape to our daily lives; we might have developed plans for the future with this person or we expected them to participate with us as we grow older. We have assumptions of how our lives work, some idea of what will happen and who will be there. Granted, this is also mixed up with what we wish for, and includes not only our expectations of ourselves but also of other people—perhaps the person who has just died. Now they are no longer here to help us fulfill these plans, indeed, to participate with us in anything. This is very hard to comprehend.

In addition, now that the unthinkable has happened, we can become very anxious about what might go wrong in the future. We are suddenly aware that another disaster might strike at any moment, only we have no idea when. Fear generates anxiety, which generates more fear.

If the death was sudden, the feeling of inability to grasp the sudden change in your situation, your life, its impact on your future, is huge. How will you manage? What will happen to those dreams and plans you had? Since this was so unexpected, you may fear that something else terrible and sudden will happen again, to someone else you care about, perhaps even to you.

If the death occurred after an illness, you might worry that this disease is in your family and will attack another person. This frightful thought can cause anxiety about who will be next. Will it be your sister? Your father? You? Many grievers rush off to their doctors after the death of a loved one, to make sure that they are not in imminent danger of dying too. Not a frequenter of the medical profession, I had a complete physical check-up after Alby died, partly to reassure myself and also for my children. I wanted to alleviate any anxiety and fear they might be feeling about their remaining parent.

If the death of a loved one is experienced as a trauma, we often have emotional reactions that are similar to trauma reactions. Startle responses to loud noises, fear of being in vehicles, worry and dread about going down a certain street or into the part of town where the incident occurred are common. The syndrome of fear and anxiety after death is similar to post-traumatic stress disorder (PTSD) symptoms, often including intrusive thoughts and flashbacks to the event itself. Ruminating on what our dead loved one felt in those last moments or rehashing how we heard about it over and over are common reactions. It's as if a huge shoe has dropped onto our lives and we are afraid the other one will also fall, shattering what is left. Anxiously, we wait, holding our breath.

Our intellect might remind us that these fears are "irrational." That may be so in normal circumstances, but grief is not a usual state of being. It smashes us with irrationality and emotions we generally did not feel so strongly before. Allow your fears to arise and, if you can, don't be afraid to express them! Later you might try applying some rational logic to alleviating some of them, by reminding yourself that there is no real threat on any particular street just because the death or cause of death happened there. There is little possibility that your brother or your uncle will also have a heart attack right away (although this does sometimes happen). Grief-related fear is a visceral consequence of the trauma of loss.

Relief

When someone has suffered for a long time with a terrible, debilitating illness, there is sometimes a sense of relief that they are no longer in pain. There can even be a sense of relief and freedom when we are released from the arduous task of caregiving. Relief can be problematic because most people almost immediately experience guilt and worry that feeling it might mean they did not love this person who has died.

Nothing can be farther from the truth. Grief is a complex cluster of feelings, some of them oppositional to each other. If you feel relieved in some way, be gentle with yourself.

Relief may also arise in the case of a complicated relationship such as in the death of a loved but overbearing and controlling person. Just as grief is complex, our relationships are also complicated. Please allow yourself to feel whatever emotion arises and recognize that all of them are part of the process.

Loneliness

A strange bubble of aloneness surrounded me when I set out to travel back home from New Mexico, two days after Alby died. Within it, I felt isolated; sounds seemed to bounce off this invisible barrier I was encased in before reaching me. I had been advised to be mindful of what I was wearing so that I could somehow be protected from strangers; when I said that I wanted to wear the silver and turquoise necklace Alby had bought me in the Santa Fe Market, Elizabeth pointed out that people might come up to me and ask about it. I said I would wear one of his sweaters to cover it but I needed to have it close to me, as if it were his hand caressing my neck.

Alone, I went through security and, by some twisted coincidence, got flagged for a body pat-down search. Sobbing quietly, I withstood it, even though our friend Missy tried to argue on my behalf, explaining to the TSA official what had just happened. The conveyer belt squeaked eerily, sounding exactly like Alby's ringtone and I automatically reached for my phone, hand instantly trembling as I realized the mistake. He could not be calling me; he was dead.

Sealed off from the world yet moving through it, I traveled across the country, struggling to maintain some composure, failing most the time. Outside, people scurried, grabbed snacks, wheeled suitcases, held children's hands, talked incessantly on their phones. I saw all this activity and felt separated from it, my blood roaring in my ears. I know I walked at a normal pace, but it felt like I was moving in slow motion. Never had I felt so alone.

Loneliness is feeling cut off from everyone, everything, even when you are standing in a crowded airport with thousands of people. Loneliness is going to a gathering of friends and feeling as if you are in a slightly different dimension than everyone else in the room. You cannot quite connect with people and at the same time, you long to join in, to unite, to feel normal again. Missing him, longing for him to come back and knowing that he will never, ever be here again to talk with, to share thoughts and ideas with— this is the meaning of bereft. Loneliness is realizing you are absolutely and utterly alone.

Loneliness arises when you are grieving, no matter who you have lost. The loss of the parent who had your back, in whom you confided, leaves you wishing for that support and feeling bereft of it. I missed my Oma so much in the months after she died, longing to tell her of my new baby's accomplishments or just about my day and to hear about hers. The dear one who has died leaves a space that is hard to fill, making you feel as if you are the one who is lost. Something happens in your day and you call out their name so that you can share it. Or you reach for the phone, suddenly stopping, your hand hovering above it as you feel foolish because of course, they are not there to call.

The emptiness of being alone settled around me like a scratchy blanket. When you are widowed, a strange phenomenon can happen to your body, so used to touching someone else, and sleeping, being intimate, holding and snuggling with them. One widowed friend had trouble sleeping because of her husband's habit of holding her hand as she slipped into dreams. She kept reaching for him in her sleep, waking up in shock that he was not beside her.

I struggled with the empty bed; I tried to sleep on his side. I tried sleeping in the middle. I ended up on my side but piled pillows, journals, my computer—lots of stuff— on his side, needing to fill the empty space. And my skin itched, not literally, but it felt overly sensitive. I could only wear soft fabric, such as his cashmere sweaters, even though it was summer. My body felt uninhabitable and jumpy. I discovered that this phenomenon has a name: skin hunger. My skin was hungry for his touch, my body longed for his length next to me, and my spirit craved his presence. Loneliness loomed in this absence, no matter how many sisters, children or friends were there with me.

Loneliness is a part of the human condition, for certainly, there have been many times in my life when I have felt lonely. I actually don't mind being alone for a time, alone with my thoughts, alone to create something. I love being alone in the kitchen, spending time preparing something delicious. I like taking walks alone, reading alone. But loneliness in grief is more like intense longing for what cannot be; a deep awareness of the permanence of absence.

It can help to be with close loved ones, even if you feel slightly isolated at the same time. Talking with people you trust and sharing stories can alleviate loneliness to some extent. Seeking out a new friend or two can also help if you are brave enough to try. Widening your circle to include others who are in a similar state, joining a support group or meeting up with other widows or others with a similar loss will offer some communion with those who understand. You don't have to go to a group; if you know someone who is also grieving, ask them to meet you for a walk, a tea or breakfast. Any activity that connects you with others will ease those isolated feelings, at least for a little while.

Consider the difference between loneliness and solitude. Within loneliness after death, there is longing for the other, a yearning for that person to fill the void. It is a kind of impoverishment created by their absence. Yet, within our loneliness and longing for their presence, there is also our solitude as we learn to live with ourselves again, without their presence. Loneliness transmutes into solitude when we fill it with remembrance and become more comfortable with being alone.

Clark E. Moustakas, a humanistic psychologist, wrote extensively about loneliness as a basic human condition. While it separates us from others in isolation, there is also the possibility of discovery. As we delve into our internal world as a result of being broken open by grief, we might find that our longing leads us to a deeper awareness of ourselves and the world around us.

> To love is to be lonely. Every love eventually is broken by illness, separation, or death. The exquisite nature of love, the unique quality or dimension in its highest peak, is threatened by change and termination, and by the fact that the loved one does not always feel or know or understand. In the absence of the loved one, in solitude and loneliness, a new self emerges, in solitary thought. The loneliness quickens love and brings to it new perspectives and sensitivities, and new experiences of mutual depth and beauty. (Moustakas, 1961, p.34)

Depression

Grief can be very depressing. Sadness, fear, anxiety and numbness are all symptoms of clinical depression, but generally the mental disorder of depression does not appear to have a cause or triggering event. The death of someone close to you does. So just as you might *feel* as if you are going crazy but have learned that this is a symptom of grief, in the same way, you may *feel* depressed at times during your bereavement. This does not necessarily mean that you need to be treated for a mental disorder. Most of the time, it is simply a part of the process.

One of the earliest explorations of the difference between grief and depression was written by none other than Sigmund Freud, in his 1917 paper entitled "Mourning and Melancholia." He pointed out the difference between what he called "pathological melancholia," or depression, and a more normative reaction to the loss of someone to whom we are attached. The emotional reactions as well as effects on sleep and eating habits are similar, but in the case of grief, the world looks bleak. In clinical depression, the person thinks of themselves as devoid of worth. In addition, depressive reactions in normal bereavement usually are transient. Be aware of this; you have a reason to feel this way and, in time, it will pass.

When you are actively grieving, life seems to have no purpose and joy has disappeared. An article from the Mayo Clinic succinctly highlights this:

> Depression ranges in seriousness from mild, temporary episodes of sadness to severe, persistent depression. Clinical depression is the more severe form of depression, also known as major depression or major depressive disorder. It isn't the same as depression caused by a loss, such as the death of a loved one... (Hall-Flavin, 2017)

Unfortunately, the medical profession does not always understand the difference between justifiable depressive feelings after the death of someone and clinical depression. They are quick to prescribe powerful anti-depressants to elderly gentlemen, weeping over the death of their wives after 70 years of marriage. Women and men are offered a variety of pharmaceutical "fixes" for what is a normal, albeit seemingly extreme, reaction to death. I am not saying that no one should take their doctor's advice, but I am pointing out that drugs can mask your feelings and prevent you from working through them.

My own doctor, an integrative M.D. who routinely uses homeopathy, vitamin infusions and other modalities in his treatment, surprised me in the fourth month after Alby's death. I went to see him because I was not sleeping more than two hours at a stretch and it was straining my ability to cope with what was beginning to feel like a hopeless life. I started crying in his office and he offered me a prescription. Through my tears, I smiled at him, thanked him and said "No." I explained that while it was very difficult for me to navigate this, I had a very good reason to feel as bad as I did. I assured him (and myself) that if I got further along and still felt awful, we could revisit the idea of using some pharmaceuticals. In fact, after two and a half years, I began having panic attacks. For about nine months, I took a small dose of an anti-anxiety medication. By quelling the panic, I was able to continue to process my thoughts and feelings more effectively as I moved towards a new phase of my life.

Again, there are reasons to take medicine and there are reasons to avoid it. Listen to your body, cope with as much as you can handle. Seek help if you are experiencing serious panic attacks: waves of debilitating anxiety that is not released through talking with a therapist or a close friend. Pay attention to your sleep patterns because sleeping soundly for a good part of the night is essential in order to function. But it is also important to recognize the difference between depressive feelings and actual depression. Clinical depression has no discernable cause. Death is enough cause to feel as if life is meaningless, at least for a while.

If you have a history of depression, please pay attention to the similarities and differences in what you are experiencing. Consult with professionals to make sure that you are coping with your grief and not triggering underlying issues. Find a good counselor to talk with, one who understands the grief and can support you.

B.A.N.D.S.: another strategy

Breathe – Sit quietly. Inhale slowly, counting to four. Exhale, two, three, four. When thoughts arise, just witness them. Breathe in, out. Do this for about five minutes, more if you need to.

Attend to your needs – Listen to yourself. Treat yourself gently. Take a walk or sit quietly under a tree. Sip something. Check in with yourself, listen to what would help right now and give it to yourself, as a little gift. When emotions rise up, go back to breathing.

Narrow your focus – Don't think too far ahead. Don't think about next year, next month or next week. Narrow it down to today, or even the next hour. Pay attention, breathe and take it down a notch.

Draw on your inner resources – You have unique talents and qualities that can come to your aid. Remind yourself what they are by making a list of them. Don't be afraid to include some qualities, even some "negatives." Anger can spur you to action and fear develops into quiet courage.

You can draw your inner resources out by writing or drawing a picture of how you feel. Make a collage that expresses your emotions. Write words on your drawings or draw in your journal. Rediscover your own resources, focus, nurture yourself and breathe.

Stay in the moment. There is no other. Yesterday is over and tomorrow is not yet here. Be present with your Self. Discover a small joy, something of beauty, a gift you received or a gift you offered. Love is a gift you share; bring that love into your heart and stay in the moment with it. Give yourself some compassion. Open to the wonderful, strong, resilient, vulnerable human that you are. Take care of yourself.

And don't forget to breathe!

Losing your mind (and finding it again)

The unruly emotions of grief can mimic depression and mental instability. People in early grief sometimes fear that they are losing their mind because of mood swings, lack of concentration, erratic reactions and random triggers – all of which are actually symptoms of grief itself.

One of the strangest emotions in early bereavement was not really an emotion at all. It was a sense that I was losing my mind. My normal way of functioning was not working; in fact, I barely functioned at all. I could not complete the simplest of tasks. Yet I had a catering business at the time with many weddings already booked, the first of which was looming on the horizon. The bride, knowing that I had been away, emailed me asking about my trip. I answered that Santa Fe was really nice and that we had seen a lot of art. Then I turned my focus on to her, asking if her wedding dress had arrived from Manila.

In the morning, I would wake slowly, my ears filled with birdsong, my heart sore and at the same time amazed that the world was continuing without him. How could those birds sing, making their nests and their babies, feeding each other, conversing in twitters and trills? Lying there in the early morning, tears would run down my cheeks, soaking my pillow. It seemed nearly impossible to stir myself out of bed.

Getting up to make breakfast and lunch, I would sometimes find myself sitting on the stair, staring off into space. Other times I would start working, consulting my prep list and gathering ingredients, only to find myself in another part of the house, not sure how I got there. I was certainly not sure what I was supposed to be doing.

Waves of emotion threatened to drown me as I flipped from rage to contortions of sobbing to vague numbness. It was as if there was some bizarre switch inside that turned on and off, flipping me from feeling to feeling without warning. One minute I would be calm and the next, nearly hysterical. Then I would have to get some work done, which seemed to take nearly three times as long.

The bottom line is, I thought I was going crazy. I could not hold a thought; I could not complete a job without having someone next to me telling me what to do or at least keeping me on task.

When you have lost your mind, your ability to think straight, what can you do?

Lists help. I made dozens of them and, if I could find where I put them, I would check off items if and when they were accomplished. The lists had practical items on them such as "call the credit card company to close his account," or "pick up child at swim practice." Items like "learn how to meditate" or "go back to school to build a new career" were on the lists too but they were not an initial priority. Keeping the fridge full of groceries and remembering to pay the bills soon after they came in were more important items. When everything felt so overwhelming, having a list filled with mundane tasks not only helped me get things done but also helped me feel less agitated. I made a promise to myself to be okay with the length of the list and to be glad if I accomplished only one thing per day.

To do list

Make a list to keep yourself on track. Here is an example of one of mine:
To do:
Get out of bed
Pay mortgage
Call my sister
Make doctor's appointment

Weed the garden
Take a walk with a friend
Take a nap
Write how I feel in my journal
Remember to eat

When you are having trouble thinking, perhaps the best strategy is to do something that does not involve your mind. Take a walk somewhere so at least your body is doing something (walking) and you can offer your crazy mixed-up mind a diversion. Notice ripples on water, notice a bunny hopping on the path ahead. Even if you live in an urban environment, there might be a park you can walk in. If not, walk the street and notice the displays in windows, the colors of street signs. Take your misery to a different place; replace your inability to hold a coherent thought with random sounds of the wind or the rustling of leaves. Find a park bench or a nice rock or lean up against the trunk of a tree. Sit for a while with no thought, crazy thoughts, random thoughts. If you have lost your mind, try to let go of the anxiety this causes. Notice where you are and just be there.

Now that this horrible thing has happened, you are deeply aware that something else equally horrible could happen at any moment. In some ways, bereavement has a lot in common with PTSD in that we are highly emotionally activated. Grieving people often startle at loud sounds, wake up suddenly in the night, have flashbacks and nightmares. Flashing back and replaying the death scene is very common and extremely unsettling. In the early days, it is hard to remember anything except the death and how you found out about it.

Living in fear expecting a calamity is exhausting. Add long periods of crying, sleepless nights, trying to wade through each day and get at least something done, and you have a recipe for losing your mind.

Finding your mind again takes time and practice. Again, lists or any system you can put into place to keep you sort of on track some of the time will help. Be gentle with your mindlessness or your agitated mind. It is a temporary condition and a symptom of grief.

I began to find my mind again through my journals. By writing down what felt like insanity, I was able to recognize how my sorrow was the cause. So I wrote down my sorrow and all the other emotions that were making me crazy. This did not make them go away but it helped me process them. My journals could hold them when my mind could not.

Coping with grief waves, monsters, bursts, numbing: strategies and obfuscations

The metaphors of grief sometimes seem like annoying clichés but these can also be helpful as frames to describe grief. By contextualizing emotions as waves, monsters, drowning and other metaphors, you will find useful ways to cope.

There are a lot of metaphors to describe the emotions of grief and many of them are apt. It is common, especially in the early months, to suddenly be overwhelmed by a grief wave which washes over you, dragging you under.

It's definitely unsettling and there is a tendency to try to repress the feelings because they are too hot to handle. The timing of the breakdown might require you to put them off for a while but I don't recommend trying to pretend that they don't exist, at least not for too long.

The best strategy for a grief wave is to ride it. When you are crashed down on the bottom of the ocean, tumbled amongst the rocks, let yourself go. Allow yourself to cry and allow yourself to float on the wave. Remind yourself that letting your feelings out is beneficial; remind yourself that you know how to swim.

Another metaphor is the Grief Monster, a dark, lurking presence that threatens to pop out of its hiding place, overtaking whatever you are doing at that moment. An elegant, elderly gentlemen, whose wife of 60 years died, said that he experienced "bursts" of grief that came in suddenly, when he least expected them. Many describe it as a roller coaster and I have to say that I hate roller coasters!

Grief is a storm; it is a maze which seems to have no exit. It is often described as a journey, which implies that there is an end or at least a concrete destination. But if grief is a journey, it has no map and the path must be slowly discovered, with many brambles and wild animals in the way.

Yet this journey through uncharted territory can be approached with curiosity. If you approach this difficult situation with a sense of wonder, as if you were a brave explorer or a hero on a quest, it might make navigating a bit easier.

> ## *Your metaphors*
>
> *What metaphors would you use to describe your bereavement? Write each one down, exploring it in detail. What color is it? How does it sound? Smell? How does the metaphor make you feel?*

For me, the shattering of my life after Alby died was a real metaphor for how I felt. Coming back to wholeness, rediscovering who I wanted to be in this unwanted but new phase of my life was my quest. But I realize not everyone feels this way. I decided to conduct a survey to see if other bereaved people shared my experience, and if not, what they thought. I asked about coping, strategies, metaphors and whether or not they felt shattered by grief.

Seventy-five percent of my (arguably small) respondents said that they indeed felt shattered by grief. Sixty-eight percent felt personally shattered and only 3 percent felt that this feeling resolved itself relatively quickly, with nearly half saying that it took longer than a year for this sense to pass. People felt that the area of their lives most affected was their sense of purpose. The next area affected was in relationships with family and friends. Most respondents felt that coming back to wholeness was an ongoing quest.

When asked about the effects of death on other areas of living, people said they felt broken in their relationships

(35%), among their friends (38%), and respondents experienced some disconnects in their careers (18%) and faith (27%). But the part of their lives that seemed most affected (82%) was their sense of purpose.

In my sample, 64 percent felt that they oscillated between expressing their grief and living their daily lives. Sixty percent allowed themselves to freely express their emotions while only 17 percent preferred to keep their feelings in check most of the time.

I asked respondents to my survey how they coped with strong emotions. Here are some of their answers:

"[I was] subdued when I was with others, but major wailing when I was alone after work, every weekend."

"There's very little choice. When it hits, there's not much more I can do but cry from a very deep place."

"I have to understand each situation that causes me to feel the true depth of my sadness. Only when I understand what caused me to return to that place can I feel better."

"I allowed myself all the emotions, but in private. It was right for me. I felt numb at first."

"I am one jumbled up ball of confusion. I've felt every possible emotion: sadness, anger, guilt, fleeting moments when I can laugh or smile at a funny memory, then pain and sadness when I realize I'll never have that again. It's been a vicious cycle."

"If I need to cry, I do. Early on, I would yell and shout out my anger when I was alone. I don't need to do that as much now but I do still cry when I need to. Sometimes it's silent tears, sometimes it's wailing out loud. But I've found I need to get it out in order to have some peace."

Denial versus acceptance

Grief work is a process and takes time. Accepting the death and the changes that go along with it also takes time, but the unwillingness to allow for the time it takes is often referred to as denial. This section discusses the multiple layers of grief, with concrete suggestions on how to navigate the pathless jungle.

DENIAL

Denial is one of the five stages established by Kübler-Ross (see Chapter 1) but I feel this term is a misnomer. Death is hard to wrap your mind and heart around and labelling it "denial" seems diminishing and somewhat contemptuous.

I deny Denial. The term gets thrown around so loosely and is dismissive of the slow, plodding experience of grief; it disavows the person who is struggling to integrate loss into their lives. I have listened to nurses and doctors label their dying patients as being "in denial" if they were reluctant to take medication which might have eased their pain (and certainly have made the medical personnel's job easier) but was against their personal philosophy or religious beliefs. I have heard supposedly caring friends claim that a griever's reluctance to "move on" is denial.

Merriam Webster defines denial as "refusal to admit the truth or reality of something…" so unless you are going around saying "He's not really dead" after someone is most definitely dead, then denial is the wrong word for this emotive state. Rather, what has been defined as denial is part of the process of acceptance.

It is true that after Alby died I had great difficulty understanding that had really happened. I knew he was dead; I was there. I watched him leave. I watched them zip him up in a black bag and wheel him out. I knew he was dead because a month later the funeral director tentatively walked into my family room carrying a black vinyl box, filled with his ashes, afraid of my reaction. I knew it in my mind and could not deny it. The reality of his death slammed me in the face with his absence at every moment.

But in my heart, in my body, even perhaps in my soul (if you don't mind that word), I did not really "know." It felt so wrong; it felt so confusing. I could not accept it on a visceral level. Was I in denial when I cried, "I can't believe he is dead?" Or was I just having trouble figuring out how to navigate the surreal reality? When a mother, grieving the death of a cherished child, says, "I can't accept that she is gone," is this denial? I don't think that is the proper word for what she is feeling. No, I think it just takes time and a lot of tears to fully integrate this new reality. It takes a lot of effort and a lot of time to fully grasp the truth of death. Rather than call it "denial," it is more like layers of acceptance that we must peel off and digest, one at a time. We may "know" intellectually that they have died, but it takes much longer to assimilate this horrible fact.

Denial is a judgmental label which leans in the wrong direction. Someone who is grappling with all the changes and myriad emotional insanities does not need this kind of judgment. Phrases like "I can't believe it" or "I can't understand it" are different than saying "It didn't happen." This last statement would really be denial. Any others are signposts along the path of grief.

People around you might misinterpret your process as denial and even tell you that you are in it. Remember that they probably mean well; they want to help but they do not completely understand how it feels to be you, inside your grief, trying to figure out how to accept it. Perhaps they have read about Kübler-Ross's Stages of Grief in a magazine or seen it on TV. There are doctors who have not really learned about grief except for these stages, who might also refer to them, thinking that this is the "right" way to move through grief. But I believe that anyone who claims you are in denial simply has no clue about what you are feeling.

Recently, a colleague came to me with a question about how to help a friend with a terminal diagnosis. In between treatments, this woman was traveling, hiking with her family, enjoying her children, taking care of her home. My colleague had a list of alternative doctors she "should" see, and stated that "she was in denial" because she was not calling them. It seemed to me to be a classic example of a kind, well-meaning outsider, looking in and deciding what someone else "should" do, rather than taking a wider view. If this patient were in "denial," she would be saying she did not have a disease and would not be going for any treatment, but would be pretending that everything was fine. Instead, perhaps she was trying to enjoy her life since she was still living it. While I applauded her friend's desire to help, I counseled caution, compassion and a little less judgment.

We all cope differently and reality is sometimes very hard to cope with. Let's leave judgmental words like "denial" and all those "shoulds" on the side of the road.

Meaning and expression

Allow me to invite you to explore emotion through expressive modalities. Artistic processes, including collage, creating a poem, touch drawing or finger painting, building a meaningful mobile or sculpture and moving/dancing with your grief are all non-verbal ways to process your emotions and help you understand your grief, your Self and how you can get through it.

Shakespeare said that we must give sorrow words, but often the emotions are so strong that words cannot capture them. By tapping into creative expression, we can explore our feelings, deepen our responses and develop meaning by making something out of our grief.

From childhood, I internalized the message that I could not draw. Surrounded as I was by accomplished artists, it was obvious that my childish drawings were not worthy of hanging in a gallery; in fact I often cringed in embarrassment if my "art" works even were hung on the refrigerator. The art I created was ephemeral—movement phrases which made my emotional fields visible through the instrument of my body seemed to move others when they were performed, but dance disappears as soon as you are finished with it. Likewise, music has the power to express thought, emotion and to tell a story, connecting the musician and the listener in profound ways. When I was young, music was a tool for social commentary and I thought it could change the world. Music is also ephemeral—at least when it is performed—and I must admit to a bit of cringing when I listen to the records I made when I was a teen, although I do admit some of it is probably better than I realize and certainly, you can hear the passion behind the song.

The ephemeral nature of music and movement is a useful metaphor for expressing grief. When we tap into creativity to release and help us understand our emotions, we are not trying to make a piece of art to hang in a gallery or even on the fridge! We are using color, shape, texture, sound and energy to make what cannot be seen visible.

You can make a sculpture of how you feel using wire, bits of fabric, perhaps a stone you collected—any object can be wired into or glued onto your visualization of yourself and how you feel. You can use torn tissue paper, crumpled up and glued onto a box, or a stick you found on a walk, allowing it to express your experience of that walk. Feathers, felt, even sequins or stickers—use anything you want to because your compilation or composition is purely for yourself. This isn't art school; this is experiential expression time.

My dear friend Deborah Koff-Chapin has developed a wonderful technique called touch drawing in which a flat board is inked lightly, a thin piece of paper gently placed on top and an image created by drawing on the back of the page with your fingers. You then peel it off, erase the image with the roller and make another. And another. And another. You can learn more about Deborah's process by visiting her website at https://touchdrawing.com.

If you don't want to take the time to figure out how to do touch drawing or if you don't have an opportunity to attend one of Deborah's workshops, you can finger paint if you don't mind getting too messy. This is a good technique for releasing very strong feelings, sticking your hands in and smearing on the page.

Once I allowed myself to draw without caring what anyone else (or more importantly, Old Bat) thought, I discovered that I really like oil pastels. They are bright and they can make bold lines. They can also be smeared or rubbed together, creating interesting smudges and blends of color. Allow yourself to explore using different materials to see what you are comfortable with.

When I free myself to use art materials to release my feelings, I am usually surprised by what appears on the page. Perhaps I made a simple spiral of three different colors but when I observe it, I see a small heart shape in the center, one that I did not consciously make. This might spur me on to write some words within the picture, expanding on what it is "telling me." In this way, I can find meaning within my picture.

Don't feel you have to save everything you make. The important thing is the process of making it, the connection between your body, heart, emotional self and, later on, your mind. You might respond to your visual expression of your inner world by writing on it or reflecting on what it is asking you to think about, in a journal. Once you are done with your process, you can tear it up, crumple it, burn it, whatever feels right. Or if you wish, you can keep a portfolio of your process work to refer to later. Just as going back to read the journals you wrote early in your bereavement, you might see some progress over time.

MOVEMENT AND MUSIC

Music always makes me want to move and since we did so much dancing in our home, it was quite devastating to realize that Alby and I would never dance again. I had trouble listening to the music he loved in the beginning. But slowly, I played favorite songs and soon I found I could move again. While it is natural for me, a former choreographer, to create movement out of feeling, putting on a piece of music you love or perhaps was a favorite of your loved one and moving your body to it is a good thing to do. It might make you cry, but that is okay.

Once I put on an old, bouncy jazz tune that was played quite frequently in our home. I was alone and happened to be in a fairly large living room at the time. I decided I wanted to dance with Alby so I closed my eyes and I imagined that he was behind me. In my heart I said, "Come on honey, let's dance." Smiling slightly, I began to move, dancing around the room, even trying to move my hips from side to side like he did. I gave myself over to the dance and began to sense him behind me, dancing with me. I continued until the end of the song, mentally thanked him and sat down with my journal.

Singing opens your throat, which in turn opens your heart. Of course, it can also open your tear ducts if you are singing along with a special song; but I don't think this is a bad thing, as long as you are not driving. If a song that feels connected to your loved one comes on the radio or you think of putting it on to listen to, please go ahead. Sing along, weep if you want to and know that you are expressing your love and are connected to your loved one through singing.

POETRY

I find poetry very powerful and am fascinated at the distillation of concepts into words, pared down to a minimum but inducing imagery and meaning so clearly in such a short space. Poetry moves me and then causes me to ponder. When I read Kahlil Gibran's line, "Your pain breaks open the shell of your understanding" (2005, p.29), I first am moved by how beautiful that image is. Then I start thinking. Does breaking me open allow me to truly understand something? What kind of shell surrounds my pain and what color is it? In this way, the poetic phrase allows me to go deeper into the meaning of my own experience of reading it.

Writing a poem to express your loss is a good exercise. You can use a phrase to start each line or begin each line with a letter of their name so it is spelled out within the poem when you look at it.

Alby

As soon as I saw him, the room fell away.
Long and lean he stood; I leaned back to gaze, almost
challengingly, at his face.
Bemused, he gazed down, the edge of his mouth
turning gently.
Yes. Everything within me rose up. Yes.

Grief poem

Write a poem about the person who died. Here are some phrases you might use to start each line or every other line.
'I think of...'
'In the morning...'
'On this day...'
'Today is just like...'
Or come up with a phrase of your own.

Poetry written by the numerous poets of the world can help you express your grief. Reading poetry is great, especially when you are having trouble concentrating, since, for the most part, poems are short. Edna St. Vincent Millay has lovely sonnets and many of them are about grief. Rumi's poems evoke love and connection. Emily Dickinson's work is concise and pure. Robert Bly's work often speaks of grief and anger from a male perspective. Mary Oliver's wonderful musings evoke the peaceful connection to our natural world and I have used her poem "Wild Geese" many times in support groups. Linda Pastan, Jane Hirschfeld, Adrienne

Rich, Naomi Shihab Nye, Billy Collins, Maya Angelou, William Shakespeare... The list is endless. If you do find some poetry that moves you, copy the poem into your journal so you will have it always.

COLLAGE

Collage is a powerful metaphor for the reparative work of grief, as art therapist Sharon Strouse discovered while grieving the suicide of her daughter (Strouse, 2013). The act of creating new images out of torn paper was a way Strouse navigated the "labyrinth of unspeakable grief," since she found that talk therapy was not helpful in the first year of grief. When your life feels fractured and frayed, what better metaphor is there than making a collage out of ripped pictures and pieces of paper? Collage is an interesting way to create images that express how you feel at this moment. Collage can also be used to work through issues of identity or to think about what you might like to do in the future.

When you receive catalogues or magazines, before you recycle them, flip through them and gather images that you respond to. If words on the pages seem meaningful, collect them too. I cut out words that seem to pop off the page and put them in an envelope for future use. I keep folders filled with pages from travel, fashion or gardening magazines. Old calendars render good pictures to use in collage. Origami paper, construction or fancy handmade papers are interesting to work with.

Personal photographs of places you are connected to or have visited with your loved one can be used in collage. Photos of you with your loved one and pictures of them in other situations in their life can be copied for use. Please don't use originals—you want to save those!

Collage

Things you will need for collage are scissors, glue sticks or the glue of your choice and a piece of paper, card stock, poster board or canvas board on which to make your collage. I like to work in circles sometimes, and round cardboard cake boards provide a good base. Mod podge or another transparent sealing medium can be applied once you feel your collage is complete.

Gather images that express one of the possibilities below or create a theme of your own. Cut or tear the parts of the images that you want to use. Ripping is good because it creates interesting edges. Also, ripping and tearing paper becomes a metaphor for feeling broken and the action of putting yourself back together.

Arrange the images on a page. When you are satisfied with your layout, begin to glue them down. You will probably adjust the layout and even the edges of the images as you collage.

When you are finished, take a deep breath. Observe your collage and how it makes you feel. If you wish, reflect on the experience in a journal.

FEELING COLLAGE
Choose images that express how you feel right now. You might respond to a particular color, a landscape. Perhaps

you have a copy of some photographs that are aligned with how you feel right now.

BEFORE AND AFTER OR PAST, PRESENT AND FUTURE

Choose images that represent how you felt before the death and other images that represent how you feel now. You can fold the mounting paper in half and keep a space in-between to depict the divide. If you wish to use the theme of past, present and future, divide your collage into three parts.

IMAGINING THE FUTURE

What would you like to do in the future? Are there places you'd like to travel to, something you want to learn? Gather images that help you envision what your life might look like, next week, or a year from now, or any time period you would like to project. Use pictures and words to enhance your vision.

CHAPTER 5

L

Learning to Live Fully Again

One of the shocking realizations after the death of a loved one is that we are still alive and they are not. Living again after death is complicated, but I believe that living fully and completely is essential and necessary. This chapter offers ideas on how to rekindle your own life, to awaken old hopes and desires and to develop new passions and interests. Living fully again can be accomplished not in spite of the death, but because of it – and because of all you have learned from being in a relationship with your loved one.

In the beginning you cannot imagine it. You cannot see how you will live again; in fact, you feel as if you are barely alive. In the beginning, when one of the important relationships you shape your life through is gone, your own life seems to have stopped. This is true no matter who the person was.

The idea that he was dead and I was not loomed large for me, like a pulsating presence somewhere above my head. As I struggled with this fact, I was acutely aware that I had to find a way to live again. I did not know how long it would take; I did not know when or even if the sense of displacement would subside. But I did know that I had to find a way to restore my sense of self, my sense of purpose in the world. The initial phrase that repeated itself in the early months became louder as time passed, especially in the second year of grief, slowly shifting from "Your life has radically changed, Now What?" to "He is gone. You are alive. How will you live now?"

Initially, just getting out of bed was an enormous task. As I awakened, the fact that I was now alone would press me down, deeper under the covers. Tears would fill my eyes, spilling out, running down my face into my ears. Once I managed to rise, I mechanically helped my teenagers get themselves together and off to school. I tried to complete a simple task such as loading the dishwasher or paying a bill or two. If I had a job coming up, I would try to organize a list of tasks, slowly, forcing myself to concentrate and complete it.

In-between moments of rote activity, I tried to imagine what my life would be now that he was no longer in it. I cast my thoughts back to things that I used to enjoy such as meeting and engaging in conversations with interesting people. Since being in public was problematic, I set this one aside. I have always been involved in the performing arts and my world has been infused with music, so I thought that going to a concert might be something I could manage. It would probably be dark in the theater, so if I started to cry, strangers wouldn't notice. If someone would go with me, it might be easier. I decided to see what live concerts were happening in my area. A nearby college had recently opened a beautiful performance space and hosts a music series based on one composer every summer. This time it was offering an evening of Dvořák, whose musical roots are in the folk music of his childhood. I mentioned my goal to my daughter, who agreed to go with me, and I bought tickets. I put on some nicer clothes, dabbed on a bit of makeup, packed up some tissues and off we went.

I don't remember the music at all; in fact, although I believe I enjoyed it in the moment, I did not remember anything about it when I got home that evening. What I do remember is a sense of accomplishment because I had gotten out of the house, done something that I used to like to do and had an activity in my day that was not addressed robotically. The music had washed over me, filling my body with a flow of notes and I had been aware of the passion of the musicians as they played. It was an ephemeral experience, one that I barely enjoyed because "enjoyment" was not yet on my list of abilities. Yet it opened up the possibility of enjoyment in the future.

This seemingly simple act of finding a concert, buying the tickets, getting in the car and driving the 15 miles to listen to an orchestra did not fix my life. It did, however, remind me that I could still function in a minimal way and probably my ability to engage more fully would increase. I decided to find a few more live concerts or shows to attend.

My brother is a professional musician who makes a living playing in musical theater. He was performing that summer in an off-Broadway theater festival, in a campy futuristic play called *The Wild Women of Planet Wongo*. He got us complimentary tickets, and my two daughters, my son and his girlfriend and I piled into the car and drove down to the City. We went to brunch in a French Bistro and rode on an indoor candy-colored Ferris wheel at FAO Schwartz before attending the show. The play was about some macho space travelers who crash-land on a planet of Amazon women who had never seen men, performed in loudly colored costumes with funny, campy lines. Best of all, my brother and his drum set were visible on the side of the stage. I remember the colors; I remember that we laughed; I remember being drained and exhausted when we returned home.

Just like the concert, even though it was a strain and a huge effort to go out and do something, I felt like I was taking important steps. I thought that even though it felt fake, I could at least pretend I was enjoying myself for a little while. Eventually, I might actually engage with what I was doing without the pretense. I decided to call this my "proceed as if" method. I could proceed "as if" I liked music. I could proceed "as if" the play was funny. The play actually *was* funny and I realized it was healthy to laugh for a while. It also occurred to me that this method of proceeding as if things felt normal was a good demonstration for us all. I desperately wanted my children to continue with their lives and to live them fully. I thought that if I could show them how, perhaps I might also learn how to live again.

Among my mundane daily tasks, I canceled some of his credit cards and was able to transfer one of them into my name. In doing so, I discovered that he had accumulated an enormous amount of points which were now mine. I realized that there were enough to take three of us to a Broadway show so I chose one and took my two daughters. Again, the daunting drive to New York, parking, finding a simple place to eat and "enjoying" the show presented an opportunity to proceed as if I was functioning. Returning home and reflecting on the fullness of the experience, I could bear witness to the fact that I still knew how to drive without accident and that I did in fact like the choreography, the music and the show itself.

I don't recommend doing too much as you try to relearn what you enjoy. I am not suggesting that going to the movies will fix your life. What I am saying is that engaging in small activities and occasionally a larger one, something that takes you out of your pain, can become a pathway towards living fully again.

I am also suggesting that it is completely normal for this to feel fake. Many of my clients have expressed that they feel as if they are just going through the motions. I know this is a strange feeling. It reminds me of learning new snippets of a combination of movement in dance class. The teacher demonstrates what they want and the class members watch carefully, moving their hands or their feet slightly to cue their bodies on what steps to take. In the dance world it is called "marking," when the mind engages fully with the movement but the body quietly simulates it. Then, when the music starts, the dancer does the movement full out.

If you are learning a song, you might listen to it several times, singing along softly until you feel confident that you know the words and the tune sufficiently enough to belt it out. If you are learning a musical instrument, you have to teach your eyes to read the music, corresponding to how to play this music on the particular instrument. Then you practice it over and over until you get it right. Learning to type or how to use new software on your computer also takes practice. In the beginning you don't know what you are doing but slowly you gain proficiency. Learning to live again takes discovery and practice.

"Proceeding as if" is like that. We may be marking our way through an activity, not throwing ourselves into it full out because we don't have the energy or the emotional stamina to do so. We may have to practice how to be in public again or even how to be sociable. We may have to try something that we used to like and see how it feels now.

How to proceed

Sit down in a comfortable spot, either inside or outside. Ask yourself this question:

"What activity makes me happy?"

Chances are, the answer for now will be "nothing." Don't worry. Ask yourself this:

"What activities did I like in the past? Am I up for the challenge of trying one of them again?"

Make a list of three or four possibilities.

> *Choose one and investigate where and how you can do this.*
>
> *Ask a supportive friend or family member to go with you.*
>
> *Go out and do it. Proceed as if you like it, even if it is very hard, feels unreal or false.*
>
> *When you get back, think about the experience. What worked for you? What was difficult? Congratulate yourself on doing it even though it was hard.*

Dipping your toes into living again is quite challenging but you can take it slowly, allowing yourself a lot of time to feel comfortable in different situations. You don't have to do this all the time; but once in a while, see if you can push your edges a bit and pretend that you want to do something that is life-affirming for you.

One new thing

An easy way to discover how to engage in new things is to try small ones, a little bit every day. Drink your morning coffee in a different cup and sit in a different chair. Take a new route to work or to the market. Talk to a stranger, make a new friend.

Practicing how to live fully again does not have to involve buying tickets or going to public events. The simple act of trying something new can also help. Experiment with doing something that you always do but in a different way. Try a new flavor of tea or a different coffee roast. Choose a different cup than the one you usually use. If you usually have your morning drink in your blue mug and sit in the green chair to drink it, make a different choice. Choose a red mug and sit in a different room. Look around at this different view and tell yourself that by trying something new, even as small as a different cup, you are learning how to live again. Notice the subtle difference.

If you always drive to work via the same route, could you go a different way once in a while? Perhaps this new way is a bit longer, so give yourself some extra time. Allow yourself to notice the different sights along the way. Perhaps you will find a new café that you could try or you might notice a flower shop you never knew existed before. Perhaps you might take this different route on your way home and stop at this flower shop. Buy yourself a small bunch of flowers or even one single bloom. Bring it home and place it in a pretty container. Notice how adding a flower to your home enlivens it.

If you are a gardener, you can bring your own flowers inside to brighten your space. Or buy an inexpensive bunch of pretty supermarket flowers; you don't have to spend a lot of money to change things a little. You can even cut a branch, flowering or not, and put it in a vase. Adding something natural and fragrant to your home shifts the energy of your space. After you have found a nice place to put your vase of flowers or branches, sit with them a while. Smell them, enjoy their beauty. Allow them to permeate your senses.

The act of trying one new thing helps break up old routines and can open the door to new experiences. In a small way, consciously sitting in a different chair offers a subtly different perspective. Notice how the room appears from this new angle and take it in as a symbol for discovering new angles in your own life.

Consider the gifts

What are the gifts you received from your loved one when they were alive? This could be something tangible; but more important, what are the gifts of the relationship itself? How have you changed and grown? What gifts did you offer and how did they help your loved one when they were alive? Consider these gifts and bring them forward into your life.

Sometimes we must look back in order to move forward. As I wrote in my journal, I reflected on my relationship with Alby and how much I had learned from it. Determined to find something positive within this terrible situation, I began to think of our life together as a gift. Indeed, aligning my life with him had provided me with a rich learning curve, challenging me to heal some old wounds and to grow as a woman.

Memories flooded me and I decided to view them as gifts as well. I remembered the camping vacation we took where everything was a hardship for me. I am not a natural camper but we had no money that year and it was the only way we could afford a vacation. I tried to think of it as an adventure, but it became known as the Vacation with a "B," because Alby threw out his back, the bugs ate the baby, birds ate our bagels and then there was the bear, who used its claw to pull our cooler out from under the table, opened it and placidly munched on some of our food. During the trip, I was tense and annoyed most of the time. Now, when I remembered it, I smiled as I see myself grabbing a flashlight to shine in the bear's eyes, while begging Alby to get the animal away from our food. It was all we had to eat for the week!

I remembered how gentle he was with our first child, how he would murmur to her while massaging her tiny feet. He showed me how to slow down and stay in the moment. He gave me the gift of love, and through our shared life— our creation of three humans, our travels near and far—he gave me the gift of growth. He gave me the gift of creating a family with a man who shared equally in the desire to show them how to be in the world while allowing them to discover their own paths.

In the early days of our relationship, we attended a two-week workshop in New Mexico led by our teacher, Elizabeth Cogburn. The inquiry of the workshop focused on long-term relationships and how to keep them alive.

One afternoon, we engaged in a physical creative conflict exercise, where partners were asked to lean in to each other with different body parts, both pushing against and supporting each other, trying to keep the contact as long as possible without falling. Alby immediately stepped in to a pose with his right arm over his head, his left arm extended towards me and his right leg lifted and bent, like an Indian Goddess. His foot flexed and he wiggled his torso, smiling with his eyes, daring me to join him in one-legged balance. I stepped up to the challenge, placing my right foot on his and taking his hand, trusting that we would hold each other up.

Can you reflect on the gifts you received from the person who died? You might bring to mind that pair of earrings or the really cool power tool you received as a holiday or birthday gift. If you choose to reflect on a physical gift, call into your mind the circumstances: how it was given, how you felt and what you said at the time. Perhaps wearing or using this object is now a way of keeping the connection alive.

When I speak of considering the gifts, I am thinking more of the intangible ones: how we shift, change and meld with those we are in relationship with. This can include those areas of resistance we might also experience in a relationship. We are not always aligned with our loved ones and relationships are complicated, often including a good amount of conflict and disagreement. These too provide gifts. My disagreements with Alby were quite loud and emotional as we struggled to reconcile our different views and different sense of timing so that we could accomplish what we wanted to in our shared life. If you are grieving the loss of a parent, you could reflect on how you chose to be different as well as what aspects of their character you might have incorporated into your Self, unconsciously or consciously. Consider all of these gifts.

An important aspect of learning to live your life fully after you have been laid bare by grief is to finally accept the good and the bad. We cannot go back and change things, so why not take a more philosophical view? I have never been a believer in that old cliché that "everything happens for a reason." However, when things were tough, I can look back and see that I got through it and perhaps took something away, even if it was to never do that again. When tragedy strikes me, as much as it hurts, I feel compelled to discover ways to make meaning from the catastrophe and to figure out how to grow through it.

I have spent time reflecting on the character of Alby, so different than mine. It is interesting that his career in electron microscopy mirrored his focus on minutiae. He understood the deeper implications of taking time to complete a task, whereas I want things done yesterday. He believed in doing things correctly; and although he never could get a grip on his paperwork, which piled up on tables and spilled out of boxes, he could wire speakers into every room and fill our home with music. We would turn it up loud and dance in the kitchen when he came home from work, swaying and bopping together, joined by the kids who alternated between dancing with delight and rolling their eyes, thinking we were nuts. That was a gift—the gift of dancing together.

Alby's warmth and empathy gave me the gift of understanding others. He was compassionate, and after he died I wanted to become more like him in this regard. Living with a man whose scientific way of thinking was different than mine gave me the gift of being open when I did not understand another person's way of thinking. His intuitive abilities which allowed him to assess a room and shift his own energy to meld with the people in it were an example of compassion that most people could not see.

Alby's understanding of me enabled me to become a better artist. When I would tell him about a choreographic idea I was working on in the studio, he would often show up with a piece of music that he found in a bargain bin or pulled out of our extensive and very old record collection. It would always be the right music for what I was trying to create, and I would never have found it myself. He could be spontaneous and fun, and this, too, was a gift.

Alby was also steady. He held the same job his whole adult life, changing with it as the technology and industry changed. He brought his intuition into the world of electrical engineering and was able to make complex machinery perform in ways it was not originally designed to do. His work ethic probably contributed to his death, but he gave us the gift of stability, which continued long after he died.

My life was enriched by his; we were lovingly tended by him. As I consider the gifts, I see that the largest one was Alby himself. I am grateful.

Consider the gifts

Take yourself and your journal to a nice place, perhaps outside under a tree you like, or on a park bench. The nice place could even be a comfortable chair in your home.

Think of your relationship with the person who has died. Consider the type of connection, the way you communicated, how you were the same and how you were different. Choose a couple or three specific aspects and make a decision to consider these as gifts from your loved one.

Write a little about each aspect. Start each part with "I remember..." and explore how this is a gift you can carry with you as you learn to live fully.

Letting go while keeping connected

It is difficult to engage in new life after the death of someone you love. Guilt, fear and anxiety often stand in the way of laughter and enjoyment. Yet we can move along in our lives without forgetting them. This section tells you how.

In the beginning of the grief process, many people fear that they will forget. As the actual sound of their voice fades, as the scent on the clothes they left behind dissipates, there is a sense of them slipping away into a void. It feels as if they were never here and yet we know they were; we can see evidence of their presence everywhere. The chair they sat in, their shoes by the door. We open a drawer, shuffle through some papers and suddenly there is an old card. I found several, all addressed to "My Beautiful Wife."

We have to find our way through the pain to live again. We have to rebuild our lives in some fashion and it would be a wonderful testament to them if we did this beautifully, fully. The problem is, we don't know how; and when we are experiencing sorrow, confusion, anxiety about what the future will hold, we lose our ability to imagine our own lives. We only see their absence and the impact this has on us.

Coming back to wholeness after grief means accepting that the hole made by their absence is yours to fill in. Some people say that they feel as if they have lost a part of themselves, meaning that they feel incomplete without this person. But if we think of absence or lack as a kind of unknown spaciousness, it might not feel quite so daunting. This space can be filled with memory, with an awareness of those gifts I referred to earlier. It is so terrible that they died, but we are alive. It behooves us to figure out how to feel complete again, even though they are no longer here with us physically.

Have you ever found something very funny and laughed out loud, in the midst of your grief, then caught yourself as if you should not have laughed? Do you fear that if you experience a joyful moment, this means you no longer care or are not grieving properly? Living does not mean forgetting. In fact, why not laugh not only for yourself, but for them as well?

Re-engaging in your own life is not an easy task. Please remember that there is no specific time for you to do this. You might have some ideas of what you'd like to do, yet you can't find the energy to do it. That's okay; you may need more time than you think.

One of my clients was beginning to participate in civic organizations when her daughter died suddenly. She attempted to go to meetings but had trouble listening, was afraid of breaking down in public and became extremely anxious. She believed that her daughter would want her to engage in her town's activities and she blamed herself, thinking she was in some way inadequate since she was not ready to accomplish her goal of being a busy, caring, active citizen.

My suggestion was that she made lists of things she might like to engage with, and then gave herself permission to take the time she needed to grieve before trying any of them. This is not an easy task for someone who is used to *doing* and who sees her value in being a productive person. It is hard to see the use in simply being with your grief, allowing it to flow, to even stagnate for a while until you are ready to try something new. How does this promote living fully again?

Being with what is happening, right now, in this moment, allows you to experience what cannot be pushed aside. Not doing until you are ready actually saves a lot of time and energy because if you push yourself too hard you may end up in a situation where you feel even more uncomfortable than if you were simply sitting at home, just being. I believe that when we focus on staying busy rather than staying present, we actually miss out on access to our own inner landscape, which is where the information on how to live fully again resides. The future may seem bleak because we cannot imagine it without this person in it, but by being with ourselves and honoring our feelings, we can learn to be receptive to what arises, which can lead to what is next for us.

Transforming your own story

We are compelled to tell the story of our grief often, but what is the story of our lives after this loss? The story we tell ourselves about our lives can actually be used to develop this newly shaped life, one that continues but without our dear loved one. Our lives after death are transformed in the telling. The story can be informed by doing new things, in trying out new activities, exploring new interests. Through picking up the pieces of yourself after the death of a loved one, the transformed story of our Selves helps us become whole again.

As I have said, I told the story of Alby's death over and over again in that first year. Once I recognized that repeating all the details no longer had the same emotional impact as I told it, I also realized that I felt a bit bored with myself as I told the story. Of course I was still devastated and sad, but I noticed that this way of telling and retelling the narrative was no longer serving me. Once I noticed that the story had dried up, I became curious. Perhaps I could tell it differently and, in so doing, transform it. I remembered something my teacher Elizabeth Cogburn used to say: that we have to be careful with the story we tell, because as we tell it, it begins to happen.

I set out to discover what new story would serve me, now that my life was changed. What would I like to create out of a new story? Consciously, I began to tell the story of Alby, not of his death but more about who he was in life. I told the story of our life together. I also began to tell the story of my survival, how I was managing to keep my household together, the kids on the trajectories of their own lives, even as I struggled to discover my own new path.

I created little personal memorials to Alby in the form of photographs around the house. I wrote constantly in my journals, allowing myself to mourn what had ended as well as to imagine a future. When I needed to accomplish something that he usually did, I made choices, either trying to do it myself or finding someone who could help me. I brought him up in conversation in an effort to keep him present and also to demonstrate to the children that it was okay to talk about him.

Longing to do something meaningful, I began to focus on how my story might help others. I started to think about going back to school somewhere in the second year of grief and investigated programs that would not take too much time or money but would realize my new goal of becoming a grief counselor. It had been a long time since I had been in school and I worried that I might not be able to perform well in a graduate program, especially since I was still having trouble with concentration. At the same time, I love learning and was a little jealous as my eldest daughter had already started graduate school. I chose an institute that seemed aligned with my view and I had a long interview with the director of the Master's program, expressing my concerns. He allayed my fears, promised support and accepted me into the school.

For me, transforming my grieving self into a grief counselor, although it took years, was a way of changing my own story. There are other ways to slowly transform the story of your loss into the story of your new way of living in the world.

Sharon Strouse, the art therapist whose daughter completed suicide at age 17, created a foundation that supports research into suicide prevention. Other people are more private, setting up a special place in their home with a photograph or two, lighting a candle and talking to the picture every morning. Some people plant memorial gardens in their backyard, with a special tree or flowers in their loved one's favorite color.

Tell yourself a different story

Imagine the story of you and the person who has died as a fairy tale. Imagine that you are the hero of the story and your relationship was a journey in which you had challenges and accomplishments, turbulent times and peaceful times.

Write this fairy tale, beginning with "Once Upon a Time..."

CHAPTER 6

E

Exploring the Past to
Experience the Future

❧

Since E is the last letter of the word WHOLE, this is the last section on how to return to wholeness after your loved one dies. But this was the first process I needed to do after my husband died, demonstrating that these different chapters can and should be used in any order that works for the reader.

❧

We are, essentially, a compilation of our life experiences. When someone dies, we are usually flooded with memories of the things we did together, what we said to each other. Ordinary things remind us of them, sometimes making it difficult to enter a room or to drive down a certain street.

For some, it is the sight of their favorite chair, now empty. The special, stainless-steel coffee pot they used each morning takes on a significance it never had before. Opening a closet and catching a familiar scent, or hearing a piece of music washes us in memory and often in tears. Delving into our shared past is difficult, but this is also where connections are felt.

Memories can also provide comfort. We can remember a funny expression they had or an experience we had in common that makes us smile as we think of it. Remembering those special moments in a shared relationship reminds us of them and also reminds us that they were alive and had an impact on our lives.

This is easier when the person who has died has lived a full life. I remember my grandparents often; their wisdom influenced who I am today, plus they lived to be 80 and 87, respectively. My siblings and I laugh about our Nana when we eat olives, remember her excoriating us when we would dance around with olives on the ends of our fingers, when she had intended them for the salad she was making. She insisted that if we ate too many, we would grow hair on our chests. She also taught me to crochet and her love of baking as well as the challenge to reproduce her famous pound cake inspired me to become a chef.

My German grandparents had a successful life until it was disrupted by Hitler, causing them to lose nearly everything. Still, they managed to carve out an equally fulfilling life once they emigrated to America. Their example of holding on to their family and embracing a new country as their own, even as they lost their livelihood, their property and their homeland, served as a model for me in the several instances when my own life fell apart. When I was cast out into an unknown world, having the path I thought I was clearly on ripped out from underneath me, Oma and Opa encouraged me to pick myself up and put myself back together again. Even though they were long gone once Alby died, I still felt that the way they lived their life was a guide for me to find a new way to live mine.

However, when we lose someone young, it is harder to use memories as a tool for connection and healing. Even Alby, dying at 50 years old, did not live a complete life, in my opinion. While I have 25 years of memory and shared experience with him, the fact that he is no longer here to see the continued growth of our children is so unfair. Our lives continue and there are graduations, careers, travel, weddings and, now, even a grandchild. He is missing so much and we miss him terribly in all these important milestone moments.

For those who have lost a child, this is an even harder task. We mourn not only the death but also the arrest of their potential. We mourn the lives they did not get to have. Yet we still have the experience of having them for that time, however brief, and recognize the impact they have on our lives now.

Remembering

Take out your journal. Choose a pen that feels comfortable in your hand, perhaps with a color that reminds you of the person who died.

Close your eyes and think of them. Relax your mind and allow a memory to arise. See this memory as if it is happening now, remembering how you felt, what was said, where you were at the time. Enhance any feeling of love or connection that comes up as you remember.

Take a deep breath, inhale and exhale. Take up your pen and write down this memory. If you like, you can start with "I remember..." and continue from there.

The quality and type of relationship have an influence on your grief and how you process it. Currently, there is a hesitancy in the thanatology world to refer to the deceased as "your loved one" because you may not have been that close, or perhaps your relationship was problematic. There may be ambivalent feelings if the person who died was withholding, absent from your life or even abusive. You still have the right to grieve this complicated relationship. In some cases, people feel a sense of relief and then almost immediately feel guilty. I believe that whatever emotion arises—whether it is longing, ambivalence, guilt, relief, rage, disappointment—deserves some process time. The last thing you need in grief is self-judgment. Take time to work through feelings by noticing them, understanding where they come from so that you will be able to release them.

For example, we don't always have great relationships with members of our family of origin. When a parent dies, problems in sibling relationships become highlighted. Sometimes it is the relationship with the parent that is problematic, that perhaps has held us back in our life choices.

Perhaps we feel that our parent never really understood us, did not love us unconditionally or was not proud of our accomplishments. Now they are dead and we don't have the opportunity speak with them or resolve these matters.

Or do we? Part of growing up is finding ways to use our life experiences to develop. Part of growing up is recognizing that not everything in our childhood was perfect and we grow through the good and the bad. Even if we perceive the parent to be the cause of some problem we experience as adults, it is our job as we mature to work through our "wounds" and heal ourselves. Therefore, if a parent dies and there are still some unresolved issues, I believe we actually can address those lingering things within ourselves.

When your child dies, are you still a parent? When your brother dies, do you still "have" a brother? If your parents die, are you now an orphan? I am still a granddaughter even though all my grandparents are dead. As I mentioned above, I think of my Oma and Opa often. In fact, my Opa was such a strong influence on my world view that I have incorporated a tidbit of philosophy from Opa as the major principle of my life. When I was 14, I asked him to tell me the meaning of life. As he was the most astute man I have ever met, I listened attentively to his answer. He said this: "Life is for learning." I knew this was true in his world, given the large collection of books on American history that he purchased shortly after his arrival in New York. He wanted to learn about his new adopted country so that he could become an informed citizen.

Oma was the first person who gave me unconditional love, which, in reflection on her relationship with her own children is an example of skipping generations. She loved her sons, of course, but her Germanic style of child rearing was different and reflected her status as a wealthy young *Hausfrau* in a fancy home with servants and governesses. With me, she could simply express her love as well as her knowledge of the world. She taught me to play Scrabble at an early age, helping me find words when I was stuck. Her knowledge of the English language was impressive, especially since she had not learned it until well into her 40s. We played many times, so that I cannot play a game without remembering her long fingers hovering over the board and her dog-eared Scrabble dictionary, which we consulted often to find legal words.

My point is that the cliché that we carry them in our hearts, which sounds so trite and irritating in the beginning of grief, is actually true. Opa has been dead for more than 40 years, Oma for nearly 30, and yet they both inform me quite often. When I bake the only dessert Oma knew how to make, I smile, remembering how she showed me how to make the crust of her plum tart with her hands and how shocked I was when she threw away the egg white. My plum tart is both a homage to her and a link that connects my past to my present. When I present this tart to family and friends and watch them roll their eyes in enjoyment because it is so delicious, I am carrying Oma into the future as well. I am literally experiencing the past, tasting it and enjoying it even as I miss her as the source, and bringing this connection into the future.

What are some of the things you experienced with your loved one? How have these changed you? What do you remember most? Your memories keep the loved one alive and can provide seeds that can be cultivated into your life going forward.

As we remember our shared experience with the person who died, we can also see that there are some things about them that we do not miss. It is okay to reflect on these as well. I do not miss Alby's terrible habit of going outside for a smoke when it was time to eat dinner, especially since his cigarette addiction was probably one of the root causes of his death. This is a hard fact, but I need to embrace it as much as I embrace all his wonderful qualities too.

The landscape of grief feels like alien territory; life is so changed that everything seems unreal. This is a good time to use your journal. Use your pen as a walking stick to support you as you explore your past. Write down a funny story, including something they said. Write down memories of trips you took together. Include what you learned from each event and begin to see how loving this person influenced who you are today. Without them, the world feels emptier and the future seems blank. But by exploring your past, you discover how to build your future.

A word for parents

The death of a child is the worst possible loss anyone can suffer. It is so wrong, so out of time and incredibly hard to find meaning, rebuild your life or figure out how to live again. Not only are you grieving the actual death but you also mourn that their life was cut short. It is hard to hear your friends talk about their children's successes, the milestone events that you will never get to experience. The younger they were when they died, the more they did not get to do. I am sensitive to those who are in this terrible position: I have children who are married and some who are getting married, and I also have clients who had children who died. They will never experience this joy.

Perhaps your child lived only hours, perhaps 10 years or 23 or 45, yet the fact that they did not live life to its completion presents a host of other issues. When Alby died, his 90-year-old mother could not wrap her mind around this fact and asked me repeatedly to tell her what happened. She begged me to tell her if there were any signs and to explain the events surrounding his death to her over and over. This was incredibly hard for me, but I knew that I would never understand the pain she felt, knowing that she was still alive while one of her children was dead.

Yet even if the life of your child was shorter than you imagined it would be (especially since our children are supposed to outlive us, not the other way around), you still have sweet memories. You probably have some stories of how they looked, how it felt to hold them, talk with them, sing them to sleep. There are memories that you can explore to keep the connection alive.

Memory

Memory is a tricky and imperfect thing. When we experience trauma, our ability to make memories in a clear way is impaired to some degree. Memories are gathered in an impressionistic way and through the filters of our developmental age at the time of the event and even if we were tired or hungry when the event occurred. Retellings of particular events also influence the memory of them. For example, my family went on a wonderful vacation in Nova Scotia when I was seven, and my father recorded this trip on several small movie reels. We loved watching our trip to "Kegeemacooch" and I cannot say if I remember going there or if I simply replay the movie in my mind when I think of this trip. Do I remember the wind on my face as we rode in the boat to get to the lodge or do I remember how it looks in the home movie, my long, black hair whipping around my small, narrow head as I smile in delight? Do I remember the story my little sister told at our picnic in the woods, or do I remember how it looks in the film, Jennifer mouthing her story while holding a strawberry?

When I remember my relationship with Alby I am drenched with richness and growth. We met when I was 24, just getting out of a terrible first marriage in which I did everything wrong. I was angry at men in general but he seemed so different. I remember how my heart dropped when I met him, as if the world had tilted on its axis. I remember how free he was in his body and how he danced with his hips swiveling from side to side. My attempts to mirror his moves caused my hips to ache. I remember how he helped me through the birth of each of our children and held them close to his heart. I remember him dancing with our youngest daughter, as she jumped on the couch wearing a cape, a pink slip with sequins on it and a hat shaped like a shaggy dog. I remember him dressing up as a court jester to take the children trick or treating at Hallowe'en. I remember his generosity and I remember his obstinacy.

Some activities remind me of him. When I was a starving dancer living in the city, he would sometimes lend me money for groceries. I told him I did not know when I could pay him back and he said, "Just pay me in pies." Alby loved to eat pie and I love to make them. Throughout our marriage, I made a lot of pies, such as blueberry crumble, blended with cooked and fresh berries that popped in your mouth. I made homey apple pies and fancy French apple tarts, laying the slices decoratively in the shell so that the whole pie looked like a flower. I made a caramelized almond honey tart from a cookbook I bought the summer we lived in Ireland. I baked his favorite pear custard tart and he would roll his eyes with delight as he tasted each bite. With each pie, I would ask him, "Have I paid you back yet?" He would look at me slyly and shake his head. "I think it's gonna take a few more," he would say.

Now when I made a peach pie with chopped crystalized ginger, I smile as I roll the crust, peel the juicy peaches, slicing them into the bowl and mixing them with sugar and flour. As I pour the fruit into the shell, covering it with another crust, fluting the edges carefully, I remember him coming into the kitchen, taking a deep breath to smell the aroma. I remember his voice. "Mmmmmm," I imagine him saying. Later, I will smile as I taste this pie. I hope the debt has been paid.

A long time ago, I sat in a waiting room while my son took a swimming lesson. A girl, about 12 years old, sat down next to me and told me her unusual name which I immediately recognized. Her wise comment on memory has stayed with me and I wrote about it in my journal.

A little girl, snub-nosed with round, bright blue eyes and
long white blond hair, sat next to me in a steamy room.
"Hello," she said. "Hi," I answered. "I am a friend of
your mother's. I remember when you were born."
"I don't remember when I was born," she said, "but you
can remember everything, if you go inside your mind."

~ (PERSONAL JOURNAL, OCTOBER 2003)

The trouble is, my mind is a very messy place. It is circular, and has a tendency to spin around suddenly, randomly landing in odd places. I can be having a conversation with someone and an event from the past will pop into my head. I might flush at the memory if it is uncomfortable, or smile slightly. The person in front of me who is telling me about his day, will note the quizzical and slightly spaced-out look that passes over my face and stop, mid-sentence, confused. I will apologize for my lack of concentration, shaking my head to clear it. I will look him in the eye to reconnect; yes, I am listening. I watch myself do both of these things.

It is like living parallel lives. I sometimes feel that split very intensely, as if I am walking through my day, completing tasks, conducting business and at the same time living the life I was supposed to have, the one that ended so suddenly and randomly in the Casa Pacifica in Santa Fe. But I have always had that slightly disconnected feeling. Here I am watching myself walking down the hallways of high school, a small figure in a dark-blue vintage cashmere sweater, a person with a loud personality who longs for stillness. Here I am in the middle of great sex, thinking about a recipe I read earlier in the day. Here I am on stage singing, watching myself from far away, a little person on a high stool, singing in a pure, too-high voice, a song about cuckoos.

When I remember this event, it comes in flashes. I sense how powerful it felt to sit on that high stool, spotlight on my face, leaning towards a large, perforated microphone on a black stand, in a theater filled with thousands of people, listening in attentive silence. As my 13-year-old clear soprano rang out and reverberated, I sense my voice traveling through the wires and into the airwaves of the radio station that was broadcasting the concert.

Memories are like this: a smell, a tingle in the belly. I have met people who caused the world to swirl around me, making everything else disappear. I have joined in a collective sound field where all of us singing knew completely that there was a peaceful way to live on this earth. I love intensely, with that same longing for soul connection, and I am told that I am too intense for this reason. Yet it is at that juncture—that shiny place where everything tunes to the same frequency, the aural vibrations align and the heart expands—this is where we truly love. I want to live inside that oscillation, knowing that we are the stuff that stars are made of, joined together by our shining inner light.

But you can't hold on to light. You can't hold on to the people you love. Even though we are all connected, no one else can complete who you are. There is an expanding trajectory through life; people grow, change, move into their own lives, which sometimes criss-cross yours again, but mostly don't. And people leave. Sometimes, they die and never come back.

Being in love versus always loving – some words for widows

What do you do with your love when your partner dies? Where do you put it? This question loomed large for me, when my marriage ended in a split second. It was an important question, albeit a very uncomfortable one because by considering it, I would also have to consider that I was no longer married. I asked myself if it was possible to be in love with someone who was dead.

Love is so nuanced; being *in love* is more than heart-racing excitement. The quickened breath, the dilated eyes, the anticipation of a phone call, a text, a meeting or a date. After a while, the passion and excitement gives way to planning a life together. Over the course of a marriage as partnership grows, being in love takes on a deeper meaning, one that includes shared experiences and shared growth. After one partner dies, what happens to being in love? Widows and widowers face a dilemma: to date again or not. Many people choose not to, feeling that they are still in love with their dead spouses. Many still wear their wedding rings on their fingers and many wear their spouse's, either on their hands or on a chain. Some have jewelry made blending the two rings into one.

One widow that I know started a relationship after six months and still felt she was in love with her husband, even as she fell in love with her new partner. It was confusing to say the least, but she persisted. Another widow decided to not date again and to learn to live alone, to continue to be engaged in her community activities and in the lives of her children. I also know a widower who married his wife's best friend four months after she died; they had become close while caring for his wife. I saw him a year or so later and asked him how they were. He rolled his eyes and said, "Well, that didn't work out very well."

No judgment here. My biggest recommendation for getting through grief is to stay with your heart (if you can feel it) and do what feels right. You may not know what will feel right, so you just have to try it and see. Plunging into a marriage soon after death may not be the wisest move because of the fog that covers pretty much all reason and thought; but if you do, it might work out. If it doesn't, then you have learned what works and what doesn't work.

Some people say they are still in love with their partners after they die. Some feel strongly that they will never re-partner. Others, even if they date again, feel unfaithful to their deceased partner.

The conundrum for me was that I felt so much love for Alby after he died, it was overwhelming. What was I supposed to do with this love? Where could I focus it?

I think love is exponential. As the mother of three, I know my love has expanded with each one and I can generate enough love for all of them; and now, as they are grown up, my love can expand to include spouses and significant others, a puppy or two and, hopefully, some next-generation babies!

What worked for me (and this may be different for you because you are unique!) is this: I know I will always love Alby. I carry him in my heart as well as in my life, no matter what I do. I am who I am because of our 25-year relationship. But, being in love is a reciprocal thing. So I cannot be *in* love with someone who cannot reciprocate, through no fault of his own. He is gone; I am no longer in love with him. And I will love him always, even after I fall in love with someone else.

Coming to this conclusion was not a snap decision. I struggled to understand what had happened to my life. I was suspended in shock, and decided to turn "How can this be?" into a long, clear look at "How it is." So my first task, in-between bouts of weeping, was to remember our marriage. Putting aside the unfairness of this, since I had not asked for it to end and we were in the middle of our lives together, I needed to put a cap on the relationship. Closure felt required. I spent a month on the timeline activity in order to relive our marriage, locate wonderful moments and banner events. I gave myself permission to look at the difficult times too, telling myself that I needed to have an honest view of our relationship. I also forgave myself for any part I played in the dark times. The best thing about the timeline was that most of my points were on the upper part of the line. Yes, we had dips, fights, financial troubles, etc., as all couples do. But this activity helped me take a long look at my life with Alby in order to have closure with the end of my marriage to him.

I drew a line in the middle of a page and started noting events, large and small, good, bad and neutral along this timeline, from the moment we met until his abrupt departure. I started my timeline from the day we met; and as I wrote down the approximate date, I remembered how I felt when I first saw him. I continued on my timeline to the date I moved out of the house and into New York

City to pursue my dancing career, to the date when Alby came to visit, at first just as a friend but then our attraction overwhelmed us and he suggested a "summer romance." My line continued through our moving in together to our little place in Golden's Bridge, through the birth of our first child, buying our first house, our second child, our second house, our third child. I included the times when we had so little money we had to choose between buying groceries or paying the mortgage. I included the time when I begged him to take a look at how much he was drinking and to stop, which he did. I included our travels, our trysts, our fights—anything I could remember went on the timeline of our marriage. This took me about a month to complete, but it gave me the gift of several important things.

1. When I ended the timeline with his death and went back to connect the events together into one line, I noticed that most of our lives together was above the neutral line. This confirmed my sense that we had a good marriage.

2. I did not have much room for regrets on my line. That was a good thing too.

3. By mapping our relationship, I could clearly see how much we dedicated our lives to each other and to our growing family. I could revel in the fact that we had done so much and with such passion and focus.

I sobbed when I got to the end because now I knew it was over. This hard fact was unpleasant but it was true. By choosing to look at our marriage in its entirety, I was able to see it in a positive way, to notice how being with him changed me, for the better.

Here is how to make your own timeline:

Timeline review

Take a large piece of paper or tape two pieces together so you have one long sheet. Draw a line in the center of it. Choose the time you want to review. In my case, I started from when we met and ended on the day he died. Write your start date at the beginning of the line and your end date at the end of the line.

Breathe. Keep breathing throughout, and get up and walk away if it becomes too much.

Think about the events in-between the beginning and the end. Begin to mark the line, putting the highlights above the line, the neutral events on the line and difficult or 'bad' events below the line. Take your time.

When you feel complete with this timeline, sit back. Breathe.

Using a different color pen, connect all the events in a wavy line. Sit back and notice the shape of your timeline. Notice how this time felt, what you learned from it, how you grew within this time. If it feels right, write about this experience in your journal. And don't forget to breathe.

A clear-eyed look at your loved one

৵৵

There is tendency to mythologize the lives of those who have departed. Wouldn't it be more honest to celebrate everything they were: what was amazing and what was not so great? This section asks open-ended questions about the life and qualities of the deceased in order to remember them with everything that they were.

৵৶

There is sometimes a tendency to mythologize the dead, forgetting their flaws and mistakes, as if we should only remember the good. I have heard widows claim that their dead husbands never said a cross word, they never had an argument and he was perfect in every way. I like to think of those I love as perfect, just as they are. And as far as Alby is concerned, it was important to see him as a whole person, with all his faults as well as his goodness. We met in our mid-20s and spent our entire marriage growing, modulating and figuring things out as we went along. We brought our past along with us, our childhoods with their wonder and wounds and some of our relationship was spent in reaction to these or helping each other override them, even heal some of them.

I cannot change the past but I might as well try to see it as clearly as I can. A clear-eyed look honors the humanity of the dead, with understanding, love and sometimes even forgiveness. Looking back on Alby clearly, I see his generosity towards others and occasionally, his parsimony.

I recall our close unity as well as the times we were like two opposites speaking different languages.

Spiritual teacher Elizabeth Cogburn says that to remember is to Re-Member ourselves. Through memory we re-integrate. When death shatters us, the broken pieces of ourselves need to be repaired. With this breaking open, everything can feel stopped, suspended in time. This uncomfortable spaciousness can be filled by processing memories, creating stories out of them, discovering truths and lessons in the past that will inform the future.

Exploring the past helps you to see aspects of your relationship to the person who has died and to consider how you have changed and grown through knowing them. Not all of these aspects will be "positive" yet this is how it was. Exploring the past can be like watching a movie of your shared life and simply noticing it. Exploring the past puts things in their place so that you can begin to consider how you want to live in the future. You can also use this exploration to decide what aspects and qualities you might like to bring forward as you reconstruct your world. I brought Alby's compassion for people of all types and his intuitive view of the world to enhance myself. I carry this forward in the work I do with bereaved and traumatized people, as I work through my own loss and stimulate my own growth. I do this because of him, not in spite of him.

A clear-eyed look at your Self

Not only is it important to process the relationship in order to move along in your life, it is equally important to account for your own qualities, strengths and weaknesses. This will help you make some decisions about how you want to live again. By considering Who you were, Who you are now and Who you wish to be, you have the opportunity to tweak some parts of yourself once you are comfortable with the idea of considering a future life.

Our lives are so often focused outwardly, we forget to look in. Sure, we are very good at taking ourselves to the woodshed when we do something "wrong," but I am not referring to the mistakes we have made in the past or regrets we might have. I am wondering if the care and kindness we offer to others could be applied to ourselves in this time of deep turmoil. If you are going to look inward, can you do it with kindness and compassion towards your own Self?

What are your best qualities? What are your "worst?" I put that word in quotations because it just might be possible that what you think of as your "bad" qualities might be, in some way, helpful to you. For instance, I have a rather fiery temper and am quick to anger. This trait has its root causes and can be hurtful to others around me, so I am still working on tempering it, toning it down and trying not to be so reactive. Yet, when I consider my anger, I can also recognize that there are aspects of this "bad" trait that are actually helpful, if I could keep it from lashing out.

When Alby died, I was quite angry. Actually, I have been a rather angry person for a good part of my life and have been trying to reduce this trait for a good part of my adult years. My anger has a lot of energy so I try to harness this energy, turning its negativity to stimulate me to action in a good way. Anger can be a motivating force, spurning me out of a funk and challenging me to use its energy to make something happen. When I lost a job due to financial cuts, I was at first very angry, taking it personally. I spent some time in a rage, steaming at injustice, feeling worthless. In a way, I had to grieve the ending of this job and I was uncomfortable with the loss of routine and loss of the focus on other people, both clients and colleagues. Even the reduction in stress was hard because its opposite was time on my hands, with "nothing" to fill it. Where would I put all this energy? Then I remembered that I had been writing for over 10 years, and now had this gift of spaciousness in which to complete this project. So my anger stimulated me to write this book.

The thing is, I have been living with myself for over 60 years and I have a big self-reflective bent. I have never shied away from personal examination, always seeking the truth within myself. Flaws and mistakes are opportunities for growth in my view, and I find that a clear-eyed look deep into myself, even if it is painful, always reveals something interesting.

A clear-eyed look at your own qualities, strengths and resilience

Exploring the past involves looking at the strengths and weaknesses of your loved one. Looking towards your own future involves discovering your own best qualities as well as being honest with

yourself about aspects of your character that could stand some tweaking or enhancement.

❧

When we are broken into a million pieces by life events, the process of becoming whole again requires honesty, which is not always an easy task. As emotional distress eases, we begin to question where we are going; as the realization that our life must continue sets in, we begin to ask ourselves what to do with it. A deep and honest look at our own qualities can help answer these questions, if we treat ourselves as compassionately as we might treat others.

Picking up the pieces and putting ourselves back together again in order to experience life fully can promote growth. As much as I wish that Alby was still here to grow with me, I cannot halt my own continuation, just because he has left. If my life is to mean anything, I must find ways to learn from his death. As I reinvent myself, I have an amazing (if unwanted) opportunity to enhance what works, develop new skills and perhaps even de-emphasize some of my personality traits that don't work as well.

Somewhere in the second year of grief, it is common to begin to wonder about the future. To some extent, our future is ours to build, but before we can figure out what to do, we need to figure out who we want to be, now.

Can you take a clear-eyed look at all the aspects of your Self? Your strengths, your weaknesses and your skills all work together to make you who you are. What roles do you occupy in life? There may be some qualities within you that you don't like all that much; that is okay. Can you see yourself as a whole being, with faults and some personal issues, but generally a person with many qualities and abilities? Here is an exercise that will help you do this:

Wheel of Identity: Who Am I Now?

Write your answers in the spokes of the wheel.
You could write a role you embody, qualities, character traits, anything that seems to answer the question. Look at all the parts of your Identity. How do they help you?

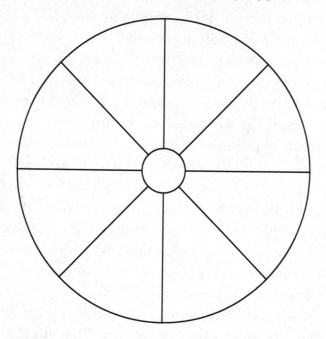

The Wheel can help you identify things you would like to engage in; for instance, you could fill the spokes with activities you would like to try or goals you might have. Then you could go back into each spoke and add a suggestion for achieving them. See this as a wish list rather than a "to do" list in order to avoid any self-judgment should you not complete it. Using a wheel to explore possibilities can help you visualize them.

The Wheel can also be used to identify qualities of the departed one, including what you have learned from each of these qualities, and even what you have incorporated into your own life.

CHAPTER 7

Grief and Transformation

Final words of encouragement

Grief is not something we can ever really "get over," but our lives can be transformed after death. We can find ways to bring the gifts of our loved ones through to the other side, where our own lives continue. We can continue to live fully while remembering them, keeping them alive in our hearts, even as we move on to new experiences and possibly new relationships.

It is said that "time heals all wounds." Rose Kennedy disagreed with this, pointing out that the pain lessens over time but wounds remain. I disagree with this as well; the wounding of death cannot really be healed in that there will always be a scar, a rift in the fabric of your life.

Just because there is a tear does not mean you will not have a life after death. As we pick up the pieces and knit ourselves back into whole cloth, we incorporate the rips into the design. In the beginning, these rips are huge, gaping and visible to everyone, or at least that is how it seems. As we slowly soothe our pain and learn how to manage it, the raw bleed of it all begins to lessen. The sharp reaction to the loss begins to soften, and very gradually, you begin to stabilize.

I have had several extreme incidents in my life that seemed to knock me off the path I thought I was on. When I was a young folksinger, I assumed that I would have a career in music. Even when the record contract I was offered by a major label at age 16 disintegrated, since I was supposed to remain part of the family group rather than become a solo act, I eventually found a way to integrate music into my choreography. When my family relationship fell apart and my subsequent young marriage also crashed, I picked myself up out of the ashes and reworked my life. So I have a personal precedence for reinventing myself, and part of my long quest to come back to wholeness included a desire to transform the pain and devastation I felt after Alby died.

I believe transforming grief is possible in most situations. While a transformative view will not fill the hole left by this death, you yourself may be able to transform, learn and grow through the process of finding wholeness again. It may be a little easier when you have lost an elderly parent. For some people, it may be a possible after the death of a spouse, whether your choice is to embrace being single or to re-partner. Transforming your life after the death of a child may seem nearly impossible; in fact, the idea of transformation, change and growth may not be a concept you are ready to embrace if you are early in your grief process, no matter who it is that has died. All the same, I have witnessed parents who suffered the terrible loss of a child long for a sense of wholeness and purpose while recognizing that there will always be a part of them that is bereft.

As we consider who our loved one was when they were alive, as we consider how our own lives have been informed, changed and perhaps even deepened through knowing them, we might also consider that we have been transformed through relationship. This does not mean that we will be "healed" and no longer feel sadness, yearning for them, wishing they still were here at various times in the future. And as our sadness lessens, as the harsh, grating emotions ease, we can witness a shift in how we feel. To my mind, this is also a transformation of our experience of grief. As we bring aspects of our loved one through into our own lives, or look at photographs and videos, and read notes or cards they left behind, we remain in an ephemeral relationship with them and this too, is something of a transformation.

Conclusion

I wish I could tell you that there will be a conclusion to your grief. I wish there was an end to it. I wish my little lavender magic wand with the plastic gems and ribbons actually worked and I could wave it around all of us who are hurting in our bereavement. I sit here writing to you, 12½ years after he died, and still I have moments of sorrow.

I miss him. I always will. No matter how good my life is in the present (and it is quite good), no matter where I travel or whatever I experience, there is always his absence in the back of my mind, in my heart, pulling at the hair on the left side of my head, as if he were sitting behind me, reminding me that he is still a part of my life. It's like a stone that has become stuck in some channel of me, and I must continue to flow around it, in spite of it and because of it, embracing the obstacle because I cannot make it go away. Sometimes this obstacle, this hard lump of matter, morphs into something beautifully luminous as I am flooded with memories of his wry smile, his warmth, his sinuous way of moving. Sometimes it just sits there and I can ignore it, even forget in the moment of doing my daily life. In the deep space of listening to someone else's grief, of bearing witness to another's unique experience after the death of someone they entwined their lives with, this weight becomes a touchstone—an energy source that helps me resonate with another person in bereavement. The touchstone can become a kind of tuning fork that hums between us, when they speak and I listen or if we just sit, holding hands as they weep and I witness.

We are born, we die. In-between we live. The people we are connected to do the same, and we hope they will have a long, fruitful, fulfilling life before they leave us. But this is not always the case and we cannot ever truly know why. Why Alby could not live as long as his father did (80) or his mother (92) makes no sense to me. And yet, there it is.

His life amounted to just 50 years. Others have less or more. But his influence, the meaning of his life, informs mine and the lives of his children. We will tell stories about him to his grandchildren who will never know him in the flesh but will hear about his escapades on his funky sailboat, *The SS Juckadoo*, when he was a kid on the bay in Connecticut. They will listen to music he loved as we do. I will dance with them in the kitchen or on the lawn or wherever we want, just as we did. He is dead but he is not erased.

As for me, I have found meaning and purpose again. I have found love again and I know this is a direct result of having loved Alby so well. I knew that I would want to be in a relationship again, perhaps even to marry again, which I did in 2015. I know myself and I thrive in relationship in spite of, or maybe because of, its challenges. My new relationship provides me with lots of love and a supportive base from which to explore the purpose of my life now, along with adventure and fun and new interests.

The Karuna Project, named for Alby, is actively helping people find their way through their own grief. I try to meet each person who comes into my office with an open heart, non-judgment and a willingness to listen. They have the ability to find their way through the terrible morass of grief and their own way back to wholeness, whatever that means to each person.

I felt that I was shattered by my loss. I thought I was broken into shards and needed more than anything else in the world to find my way back to feeling whole again. As I processed my grief and helped my children heal and continue on their paths, I sought my own path forward, carrying parts of Alby with me. And along the way, I found that I was never really broken.

Grief shattered me, but by discovering that I was never really broken, that I was always intrinsically wholly me, I have shattered grief.

References

Coloroso, B. (2000). *Parenting through Crisis: Helping Kids in Times of Loss, Grief and Change.* New York: HarperCollins.

cummings, e.e. (1954). *100 Selected Poems.* New York: Grove Press.

Didion, J. (2006). *The Year of Magical Thinking.* New York: Alfred A. Knopf.

Freud, S. (1957). 'Mourning and Melancholia'. In *The Standard Edition of the Complete Psychological Works of Sigmund Freud, Volume XIV.* Trans. J. Strachey. London: The Hogarth Press. [Original work published 1917.]

Gibran, K. (2005). *The Prophet.* New York: Alfred A. Knopf.

Hall-Flavin, D.K. (2017). *Mayo Clinic: Diseases and Disorders.* Retrieved from Mayo Clinic on 5/12/2017: www.mayoclinic.org/diseases-conditions/depression/expert-answers/clinical-depression/faq-20057770

Kübler-Ross, E. and Kessler, D. (2005). *On Grief and Grieving.* New York: Scribner.

Lewis, C.S. (1961). *A Grief Observed.* London: Faber.

Lichtenthal, W. (2017, April). *When those who need it most use it least: Facilitating grief support for those at greatest risk.* Keynote lecture presented at the Association of Death Education and Counseling Conference, Portland, Oregon.

Moustakas, C.E. (1961). *Loneliness.* Upper Saddle River, NJ: Prentice Hall.

Neimeyer, R.A. (2012a). 'Correspondence with the Deceased.' In R.A. Neimeyer (ed.) *Techniques of Grief Therapy: Creative Practices for Counseling the Bereaved.* New York: Routledge.

Neimeyer, R.A. (2012b). 'Retelling the Narrative of the Death.' In R.A. Neimeyer (ed.) *Techniques of Grief Therapy: Creative Practices for Counseling the Bereaved.* New York: Routledge.

Orloff, J. (2010). 'The Health Benefits of Tears.' Retrieved from *Pyschology Today* on 5/12/2017: www.psychologytoday.com/blog/emotional-freedom/201007/the-health-benefits-tears

Pennebaker, J.W. (1997). *Opening Up: The Healing Power of Expressing Emotions.* New York: Guilford Press.

Pennebaker, J.W. and Evans, J.F. (2014). *Expressive Writing: Words That Heal.* Eumenclas, WA: Idyll Arbor, Inc.

SARK (2010). *Glad No Matter What: Transforming Loss and Change into Gift and Opportunity.* Novato, CA: New World Library.

Sarton, M. (1973). *Journal of Solitude.* New York: W.W. Norton.

Silverman, P. (2017). *Living with Grief: Children, Adolescents and Loss.* Accessed on January 31, 2018 at www.phyllisrsilverman.com/articles.html

Stroebe, M. and Schut, H. (1999). The Dual Process Model of Coping with Bereavement: Rationale and Description. *Death Studies, 23*(3), 197–224.

Strouse, S. (2013). *Artful Grief: A Diary of Healing.* Bloomington, IN: Balboa Press.

Wolfelt, A.D. (2003). *Understanding Your Grief: Ten Essential Touchstones for Finding Hope and Healing Your Heart.* Fort Collins, CO: Companion Press.

Worden, J.W. (2009). *Grief Counseling and Grief Therapy.* New York: Springer Publishing.